OECD Reviews on Local Job Creation

Employment and Skills Strategies in Poland

OECD
BETTER POLICIES FOR BETTER LIVES

LEED
BUILDING MORE & BETTER JOBS

Please cite this publication as:
OECD (2016), *Employment and Skills Strategies in Poland*, OECD Reviews on Local Job Creation, OECD Publishing, Paris.
http://dx.doi.org/10.1787/9789264256521-en

ISBN 978-92-64-25549-4 (print)
ISBN 978-92-64-25652-1 (PDF)

Series: OECD Reviews on Local Job Creation
ISSN 2311-2328 (print)
ISSN 2311-2336 (online)

Photo credits: © Andy Dean Photography/Shutterstock.com, © Pakhnyushchy/Shutterstock.com.

Corrigenda to OECD publications may be found on line at: *www.oecd.org/publishing/corrigenda*.

Preface

The year 2016 is the 20th anniversary of Poland's membership in the OECD. During this time, Poland has shown impressive economic growth and improvement in well-being. Poland was one of the few OECD countries in which growth remained positive during the financial crisis. While growth has rebounded from the abrupt slowdown in 2012-13, Poland's low employment rate hinders prospects for future growth going forward. Like its peers in the OECD, Poland is grappling with how to create jobs in sufficient quantities and of sufficient quality to move towards a path of strong and resilient growth.

Over recent years, the work of the OECD LEED Programme on *Designing Local Skills Strategies*, *Building Flexibility and Accountability into Local Employment Services*, *Breaking out of Policy Silos*, *Leveraging Training and Skills Development in SMEs*, and *Skills for Competitiveness* has demonstrated that local strategies to boost skills and job creation require the participation of many different actors across employment, training, economic development, and social welfare portfolios. Employers, unions and the non-profit sector are also key partners in ensuring that education and training programmes provide the skills needed in the labour markets of today and the future.

The *OECD Reviews on Local Job Creation* deliver evidence-based and practical recommendations on how to better support employment and economic development at the local level. This report builds on sub-national data analysis and consultations at the national level and with local stakeholders in two case study areas. It provides a comparative framework to understand the role of the local level in contributing to more and better quality jobs. The report can help national, regional and local policy makers in Poland build effective and sustainable partnerships at the local level, which join-up efforts and achieve stronger outcomes. Co-ordinated policies can help workers find suitable jobs, while also stimulating entrepreneurship and productivity, which increases the quality of life and prosperity within a community as well as throughout the country.

I would like to warmly thank the Ministry of Economic Development for their active participation and support of the study, as well as the Ministry of Family, Labour and Social Policy for their ongoing contributions.

Mari Kiviniemi,
Deputy Secretary-General, OECD

Foreword

This review was undertaken by the Local Economic and Employment Development (LEED) Programme of the Organisation for Economic Co-operation and Development (OECD) as part of a project undertaken in co-operation with the Ministry of Economic Development, and with the support of the Ministry of Family, Labour and Social Policy. This project is part of the OECD LEED programme of work under the leadership of Sylvain Giguère.

The principal authors are Piotr Stronkowski (independent consultant), Anna Rubin (Policy Analyst, OECD) and Jonathan Barr (Policy Analyst, OECD). The authors would like to thank Michela Meghnagi, Angela Attrey, and Pierre Georgin for their work on the data analysis, as well as François Iglesias, Barbara Cachova, and other colleagues in the OECD LEED Programme for their assistance with this project.

The authors would also like to acknowledge the valuable contributions of Prof. Steve Johnson (University of Hull) for his participation on the project study visit as well as Joanna Obarymska-Dzierzgwa, Przemyslaw Herman (Ministry of Economic Development) and Ewa Rastenska (Ministry of Family, Labour and Social Policy) for their participation in this project.

Finally, special thanks are given to the national and local representatives who participated in the project interviews and roundtables, and provided documentation and comments critical to the production of the report.

Table of contents

Tables

Figures

Reader's guide

The *Local Job Creation* project involves a series of country reviews in Australia, Belgium (Flanders), Canada, Czech Republic, France, Ireland, Israel, Italy (Autonomous Province of Trento), Korea, Poland, Slovenia, Sweden, Turkey, the United Kingdom and the United States (California and Michigan). The key stages of each review are summarised in Box 1.

Box 1. **Summary of the OECD LEED Local Job Creation Project Methodology**

- Analyse available data to understand the key labour market challenges facing the country in the context of the economic recovery and apply an OECD LEED diagnostic tool which seeks to assess the balance between the supply and demand for skills at the local level.
- Map the current policy framework for local job creation in the country.
- Apply the local job creation dashboard, developed by the OECD LEED Programme (Froy et al, 2010) to measure the relative strengths and weaknesses of local employment and training agencies in contributing to job creation.
- Distribute an electronic questionnaire to local labour offices (poviat labour offices in Poland) to gather information on how they work with other stakeholders to support local job creation policies.
- Conduct an OECD study visit, where local and national roundtables with a diverse range of stakeholders are held to discuss the results and refine the findings and recommendations.
- Contribute to policy development in the reviewed country by proposing policy options to overcome barriers, illustrated by selected good practice initiatives from other OECD countries.

While furthering the recovery from the economic crisis remains a focus of policy-makers, there is a need for both short-term and longer-term actions to ensure sustainable economic growth. In response to this issue, the OECD LEED Programme has developed a set of thematic areas on which local stakeholders and employment and training agencies can focus efforts. These include:

1. **Better aligning policies and programmes to local economic development** challenges and opportunities;
2. **Adding value through skills:** Creating an adaptable skilled labour force and supporting employment progression and skills upgrading;
3. **Targeting policy to local employment sectors and investing in quality jobs,** including gearing education and training to emerging local growth sectors and responding to global trends, while working with employers on skills utilisation and productivity; and,
4. **Being inclusive** to ensure that all actual and potential members of the labour force can contribute to future economic growth.

Local Job Creation Dashboard

As part of the project, the LEED Programme has drawn on its previous research to develop a set of best practice priorities in each thematic area, which is used to assess local practice through the local job creation dashboard (see Box 2). The dashboard enables national and local policy-makers to gain a stronger overview of the strengths and weaknesses of the current policy framework, whilst better prioritising future actions and resources. A value between 1 (low) to 5 (high) is assigned to each of the four priority areas corresponding to the relative strengths and weaknesses of local policy approaches based on best practices in other OECD countries.

Box 2. **Local Job Creation Dashboard**

Better aligning policies and programmes to local economic development

1.1. Flexibility in the delivery of employment and vocational training policies

1.2. Capacities within employment and VET sectors

1.3. Policy co-ordination, policy integration and co-operation with other sectors

1.4. Evidence based policy making

Adding value through skills

2.1. Flexible training open to all in a broad range of sectors

2.2. Working with employers on training

2.3. Matching people to jobs and facilitating progression

2.4. Joined up approaches to skills

Targeting policy to local employment sectors and investing in quality jobs

3.1. Relevance of provision to important local employment sectors and global trends and challenges

3.2. Working with employers on skills utilisation and productivity

3.3. Promotion of skills for entrepreneurship

3.4. Promoting quality jobs through local economic development

Being inclusive

4.1. Employment and training programmes geared to local "at-risk" groups

4.2. Childcare and family friendly policies to support women's participation in employment

4.3. Tackling youth unemployment

4.4. Openness to immigration

The approach for Poland

This study has looked at the range of institutions and bodies involved in workforce and skills development in Poland. In-depth analysis based on document reviews and interviews with key stakeholders was undertaken to look at local employment and economic development activities in two geographic regions:

- the Radomski sub-region; and
- the Poznań sub-region.

In each case study area, interviews were conducted with a wide set of stakeholders. An electronic questionnaire was also sent to managers of poviat labour offices across Poland, which requested information on their management, capacities, and activities. The questionnaire was administrated during the summer of 2015 and the results are based on 208 valid responses (see Appendix A). In July 2015, local roundtables were held in each of the case study areas and at the national level to discuss the findings and recommendations. These meetings brought together a range of stakeholders, including relevant department officials in the fields of employment, economic development, and training; employers; and other local community and social development organisations.

References

Froy, F., S. Giguère and E. Travkina (2010), *Local Job Creation: Project Methodology*, OECD Local Economic and Employment Development (LEED), OECD, Paris, *www.oecd.org/cfe/leed/Local%20Job%20Creation%20Methodology_27%20February.pdf*.

Abbreviations and acronyms

ESF	European Social Fund
Gmina	Community/municipality
IVET	Initial vocational education and training
LCO	Qualifying vocational course
LEED	Local Economic and Employment Development Programme
OECD	Organisation for Economic Co-operation and Development
NQF	National Qualification Framework
MLSP	Ministry of Labour and Social Policy (now Ministry of Family, Labour and Social Policy)
PAI	Activation and Integration Programme
PES	Public employment services
Poviat	County level of government
PQF	Polish Qualifications Framework
SEZ	Special economic zone
VET	Vocational education and training
Voivodeship	Regional level of government
ZUS	Social Insurance Institution

Executive summary

Since 2000, Poland has steadily caught up with the EU15 in terms of GDP-per-capita and is one of the few OECD countries where growth remained positive during the financial crisis. However, in 2012-13 the economy abruptly slowed down, and employment remains a major structural weakness. Poland has a particularly low employment rate, and ranks poorly compared to other OECD countries on measures of job quality, such as wages and overall job security.

The OECD Local Economic and Employment Development (LEED) programme has developed its reviews on Local Job Creation as an international comparative study to examine the contribution of local labour market policy to boosting quality employment and productivity. To help Poland respond to the challenges it faces, the review has looked at a range of institutions and bodies involved in employment and skills policies. In addition to reviewing national policies, in-depth work was undertaken in the first half of 2016 in two Polish sub-regions to assess implementation and service delivery capacity: the city of Poznań and the Radomski sub-region.

Overall, the review found that while many of the necessary mechanisms are in place in Poland to allow local actors to tailor policies to local needs, these mechanisms are often undermined by low capacity and lack of strong "conveners" to bring together public actors with employers to form partnerships for better employment and job creation outcomes. However, successful examples of how stakeholders have overcome these barriers can be found, and initiatives such as the National Training Fund and the establishment of sector councils offer promise going forward. The following key conclusions and recommendations are intended to help build and expand on the recent and ongoing reforms to strengthen the role of local actors in boosting job creation.

Key conclusions and recommendations

Better aligning programmes and policies to local economic development

- **Carefully monitor the reforms to the public employment service (PES) and adjust as necessary to prevent unintended consequences.** In particular, attention should be paid to the new system of performance management to reduce incentives to "game" the system (e.g. through creaming), and to create mechanisms to adjust performance metrics based on local conditions and priorities.
- **Improve local co-ordination of employment and skills policies and programmes.** Local labour market councils play this role to some degree, but in many cases, lack the capacity, strategic leadership and/or statutory authority to effectively bring together and guide the various actors.
- **Increase the availability and use of data at the sub-national level and build a stronger evaluation culture.** Strengthening the capacities and methodologies used by the

Regional Labour Market Observatories, using longer-term outcomes to measure the success of labour market programmes, better leveraging data available through Social Insurance Institutions, and enhancing the quality and use of evaluations can all contribute to improving the use of evidence.

Adding value through skills

- **Make the VET system more responsive to local labour market needs, including through better engagement of employers.** A key gap identified was a misalignment between the VET system and local labour market needs. Increasing employer engagement at the strategic level (i.e. in steering local decision-making related to VET) as well as in the day-to-day practicalities of offering work-based learning opportunities could help to close this gap.
- **Expand offerings to improve basic skills.** While there is a clear need to improve the level of basic skills in Poland, relatively few programmes offer this type of training. Ensuring that VET and training institutions include more focus on improving basic and generic skills should be complemented by remediation courses to reach those already outside the training and education system.

Targeting policy to local employment sectors and investing in quality jobs

- **Focus on improving skills utilisation and work organisation.** More attention has been recently paid to questions around job quality, but an overlooked aspect is considering how employers are using skills of those already employed. There may be opportunities for the public sector to use instruments such as the National Training Fund to engage more with employers around increasing the demand for and use of skills.
- **Promote economic development that is inclusive and contributes to the creation of quality jobs, including through more strategic use of public procurement.** More consideration should be given to the quality of jobs created through economic development efforts, not just the quantity. Additionally, local authorities could use social clauses in public procurement to promote quality jobs and the inclusion of disadvantaged populations in the labour market.
- **Ensure that adequate guidance and information on career pathways are available to both youth and adults, and that it is informed by local labour market assessments.** Most study participants agreed that current career guidance provided to youth and adults is inadequate. Delivering high quality career guidance requires having dedicated and competent staff that have access to up-to-date information on both national and local labour markets.

Being inclusive

- **Address gaps in services for the most disadvantaged clients of the public employment service.** While the introduction of a profiling mechanism as part of the PES reforms can help in targeting resources more strategically, in practice, its implementation has created a gap in services for the most disadvantaged clients. Focused attention should be paid to addressing this gap quickly.
- **Improve access to child care services, particularly for children aged 0-3 years of age.** Improving the overall availability and quality of child care has been identified by the government as a priority. The significant improvements in providing access to affordable care and quality services will need to be furthered.

Chapter 1

Policy context for employment and skills in Poland

This chapter provides an overview of Poland's employment and skills system and the economic context. Poland was one of the few OECD countries where GDP growth remained positive during the financial crisis. While it experienced an abrupt slowdown in 2012, growth is now back on a solid path. Compared to other OECD countries, responsibility for labour market policies and vocational education and training are relatively decentralised, and important reforms have been implemented in both policy areas in recent years.

Economic and labour market trends

Since 2000, Poland has steadily caught up with the EU15 in terms of GDP-per-capita and was one of the few OECD countries where growth remained positive during the financial crisis. While growth abruptly slowed in 2012-13 due to a number of factors (a fall in public investment; weak external demand; and rising unemployment and fiscal consolidation that dampened household consumption) (OECD, 2014a), it is now back on a solid path (estimated to be 3.5% in 2016-17) (OECD, 2016a).

Figure 1.1. **GDP growth rate, OECD and Poland, 2006-14**

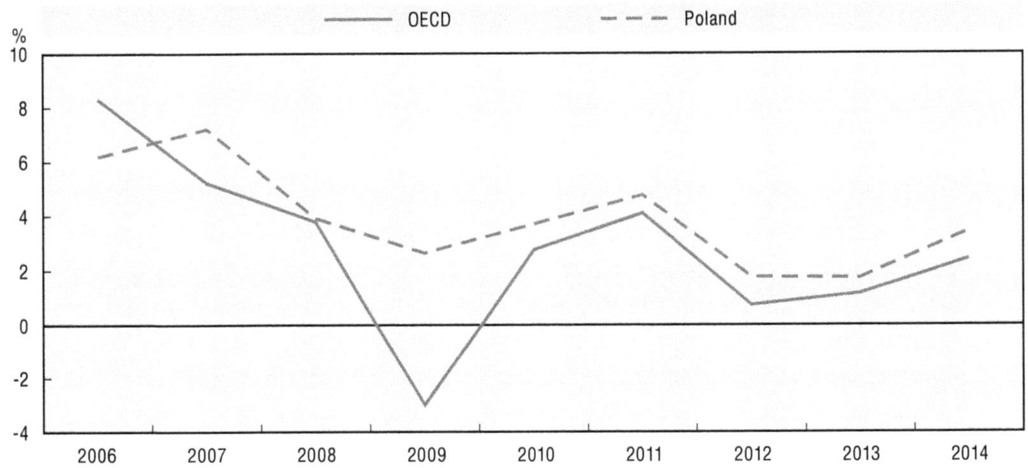

Source: OECD (2014b), "Aggregate National Accounts: Gross domestic product", *OECD National Accounts Statistics* (database), *http://dx.doi.org/10.1787/data-00001-en.*

Poland's unemployment and employment rates have improved in recent years, but labour market challenges persist (OECD, 2016a). At 63.0% in the third quarter of 2015 (OECD, 2016b), Poland's employment rate ranks at the low end of OECD countries. The national unemployment rate slowly increased in the period between 2009 and 2013, although it has since started to decrease again. As of the third quarter of 2015, Poland's unemployment rate was 7.4%, somewhat higher than the OECD average (6.7%) (OECD, 2016c).

Poor labour market outcomes are particularly marked at both ends of the age spectrum. The labour force participation rate for workers aged 55 to 64 was 45.6% in 2014, compared to an OECD average of 60.5% (OECD, 2016d). At the other end of the age spectrum, youth unemployment increased from 20.7% in 2009 to 23.9% in 2014. This is significantly higher than the OECD average of 15% in 2014 (OECD, 2016e). There is wide regional variation in youth unemployment rates in the same year but even the lowest figure – Mazovia at 17.7% – is higher than the 2014 OECD average (OECD, 2016f).

There are also significant gender differences in employment rates: 69% of the male labour force was employed in Q3 2015 compared to 57% of the female labour force (OECD,

2016a). The OECD has identified poorly designed family and pension policies as key contributors to low female employment rates (OECD, 2014a).

Boosting employment prospects is critical given that Poland will be facing strong population shrinkage. It has low fertility rates and a quickly ageing population structure. Emigration also contributes to demographic change: in 2007 there were an estimated 2.3 million Polish citizens, or 6% of the total population, staying temporarily abroad, compared to 1.0 million in 2004 (OECD, 2014a). Additionally, compared to other OECD countries, Poland receives very few migrants each year, and is thus unable to offset these decreases in the labour supply with increased migration.

Almost one quarter (22.2%) of people employed in Poland worked in the distributive trade, repairs, transport, accommodation and food service activities. Nearly the same share of employed (18.9%) worked in manufacturing, while 20.4% were employed by the public sector in 2014 (OECD, 2014c). Agriculture, forestry and fishing workers only comprised 11.4% of the total, although this is higher than in most OECD countries. These four sectors together give almost 73% of the total employment in Poland.

Poland also has the highest rate of workers on temporary contracts in the European Union, which undermines productivity and well-being (OECD, 2016a). While difficult to measure, it is also worth noting that the size of the informal economy in Poland is probably high relative to other OECD countries (Andrews et al., 2011).

Finally, attainment of upper secondary and tertiary education has been steadily increasing in Poland. First-time graduation rates at the upper secondary level increased from 41% to 86% between 2005 and 2013, with Poland now having one of the highest upper secondary graduation rates in the OECD (OECD, 2015). However, PIAAC results show that Poland's mean literacy and numeracy scores are low in comparison to other participating countries, although these results may be largely generational, as Poland's scores are closer to the participating countries' average for younger adults (16-24 year olds) (OECD, 2013).

Overview of employment policies and programmes*

PES have a long history in Poland. After 1989, a system of public employment services was established with three operational levels: the national Labour Office, regional labour offices and poviat (local) labour offices. In 1999, Public Employment Services in Poland were decentralised. The National Labour Office was liquidated and some of its responsibilities were transferred to the Ministry of Labour and Social Policy. Poviat labour offices became part of local government at the district level (poviat), while regional labour offices became part of the regional government (voivodeship). As a result, there are now three level of PES in Poland:

- Poviat labour offices – responsible for providing benefits to unemployed persons and implementing active labour market policy instruments;
- Regional labour offices – responsible for analysis, strategic planning, and services for specific groups; and

* In 2015, the Ministry of Labour and Social Policy was reconfigured as the Ministry of Family, Labour and Social Policy and the Ministry of Infrastructure and Development and the Ministry of Economy were joined to form the Ministry of Economic Development. The ministries are referred to by their new names throughout this publication except in reference to actions taken prior to 2015.

- Ministry of Family, Labour and Social Policy – responsible for the legislative framework, national strategy, managing the Labour Fund, and financing active labour market policies.

These three tiers are independent, with no hierarchical relationship between them. Local government is responsible for financing the operational costs of poviat labour offices, while benefits for the unemployed and active labour market policy measures are financed by the Labour Fund. This Fund is part of the national budget, which is distributed by the Ministry of Family, Labour and Social Policy to regional labour offices and then distributed to poviat labour offices. Labour market councils operate at each governance level, although they largely play an advisory role and their actual influence on programme and policy decisions varies.

The 1999 reform gave more autonomy to poviat labour offices and more opportunities to coordinate actions related to the local labour market, as local authorities at the poviat level are also responsible for other policy areas relevant to the labour market (e.g. secondary education, including vocational education; more specialised social assistance services, including support for disabled persons). While this reform was intended to result in a higher level of co-ordination between labour market policies and other locally managed policy areas, not all local authorities have taken advantage of these opportunities. According to research conducted in 2008, a significant proportion of local authorities did not engage in solving labour market problems and treated PES as separate offices, not as an important element of a comprehensive development policy (MLSP, 2008).

The financial crisis brought about significant challenges for public employment services. The number of unemployed persons started to grow. At the same time, the Government decided to significantly reduce funds for active labour market policies due to fiscal constraints. This temporarily decreased the PES' ability to respond to the crisis on the labour market.

In 2012, the Ministry of Labour and Social Policy proposed significant reforms of the PES. The main objectives of the reform were to improve the effectiveness of active labour market policies; improve the quality of services provided by PES; and improve the targeting of active labour market policies. The reform was introduced in 2014, with the following main changes:

- **The distribution of the Labour Fund will now partially depend on the effectiveness of labour offices.** The effectiveness of the labour office was added as a new variable to the algorithm defining the allocation of financing from the Labour Fund.

  Additionally, staff of poviat labour offices who achieve targets above the average for all labour offices will receive bonuses financed from the Labour Fund. Up to 2% of the Labour Fund will be allocated to this mechanism. There are three main indicators taken into account:

  - Number of client advisors working with the unemployed;
  - Effectiveness – percentage of unemployed taking part in active labour market policy measures and/or placed in employment; and
  - Efficiency – the unit cost of active labour market policy instruments.

- **Profiling to target support for the unemployed has been introduced.** This measure was intended to help better target services. In this context, it is worth noting that a large concern in Poland is that some people registered as unemployed are in fact not really interested in actual assistance.[1] In an internal publication, the MLSP estimates that such persons account for 30-40% of all registered unemployed. As a result – according to the

Ministry of Family, Labour and Social Policy – labour offices devote insufficient resources to working with an improperly defined target group (MLSP, 2014). Therefore, three profiles were introduced to better target active labour market policies. These profiles were based on two variables: availability of the unemployed for work and distance of the unemployed from the labour market.

- Profile I – a person close to the labour market and ready to return to work;
- Profile II – an average willingness to work and an average distance away from the labour market; and
- Profile III – persons far away from the labour market or not ready to become employed.

Profile I persons are perceived as not needing intensive support and able to solve their problems alone or with limited, basic assistance. Therefore, their support is limited to job placement, career counselling and selected labour market services. Reducing support for this group decreases the negative effect of dead-weight (providing assistance to those who would manage to find a job without support).

Persons assigned to the second profile are acknowledged as the key clients of labour offices – persons for whom it would be difficult to become employed on their own, but are motivated enough to change their situation. In other words, the services and labour market instruments are particularly beneficial for them.

Profile III – distant from the labour market – represents persons whose problems are serious and complex and cannot be solely addressed by the labour office. These persons may need more intense and long-term support (e.g. counselling and support). Labour offices may not have the tools or resources to carry out this type of intensive and personalised support. Therefore, the activation of these persons is outsourced to external groups (employment agencies, social assistance centres or NGOs) working within the framework of a new instrument: the Activation and Integration Programme (PAI).

- **Outsourcing activation services.** From a legal point of view, poviat labour offices have been able to outsource activation measures for many years, but the regulation has not been applied. This is mostly due to a lack of interest on the part of poviat labour offices, as well as the unattractive contractual terms for potential service providers. Currently, according to the amendment to the law, outsourcing is able to take place at the regional level. The remuneration for the contractor depends on its performance (number of unemployed placed in jobs and employment retention rates).

  The new regulation on outsourcing is intended to improve the effectiveness of employment services (based on the assumption that specialised institutions are more effective at working with the "most difficult" cases), as well as strengthening regional partnerships. It should promote better co-ordination of activities for the unemployed in the region.

- **Changed organisation of work in poviat labour offices.** This includes the introduction of a new position: a client advisor who is responsible for managing the whole process of activating the unemployed. A similar mechanism was created for employers through the introduction of an institutional client advisor position.
- **National Training Fund.** This fund is a new instrument (financed by the Labour Fund), that supports the development of employees' skills. The instrument is addressed to small and medium enterprises. During 2014-15, this support will be targeted to employees over 45 years of age.

- **New instruments of active labour market policies.** The new legislation introduced a number of new instruments, widening the scope of services provided by PES.

It is too early to assess the results of the reforms, although some elements have been already discussed. More in-depth analyses of particular elements of the reform are presented in a further section of this report. It is worth mentioning here, however, that the most controversial change is the profiling. This mechanism, designed by the Ministry of Family, Labour and Social Policy, significantly reduces the autonomy and flexibility of the professionals at poviat labour offices. This results in increased resistance to the change. Another controversy concerns the third profile – even though it was assumed that assistance centres would provide services to the person categorised to the third profile, most assistance centres are not interested in implementing PAI due to a lack of resources. As a result, persons who are placed into this profile in fact have limited access to the appropriate support.

Public Employment Services are not the only actors in the field of labour market policies. Although Public Employment Services play a central role, other institutions are also active in this area, such as:

- Voluntary Labour Corps – part of the government administration, responsible for supporting adolescents over 15 years of age and unemployed persons under 25 years of age to prevent them from dropping out of the educational system and becoming unemployed;
- Employment agencies – non-public institutions, responsible for recruitment, including recruiting for work abroad with foreign employers, vocational guidance, counselling, and temporary employment;
- Training institutions – institutions providing training and education (outside of formal education);
- Institutions of social dialogue – trade unions, organisations of employers, non-governmental organisations working in the field of the labour market;
- Local partnership institutions.

Another relevant institution in Poland are social assistance centres. Social assistance centres operate at the lowest level of local government (gmina – community). Social assistance centres provide social benefits, social work and social services for people facing the most difficult life situations. However, the largest group of its clients are unemployed people. Thus, in practice, the social assistance and poviat labour offices often work with the same clients.

Finally, since 2004, the European Social Fund (ESF) has significantly supported labour market policies in Poland. Each ESF budget has a considerable allocation of funds available to poviat labour offices. As a result, each poviat labour office implements projects financed by the ESF. In practice, the ESF finances the regular activities of local offices; however, additional funding allows the scope of active labour market policies to be extended.

The ESF also finances projects implemented by other organisations working in the field of labour market policies: social assistance centres, NGOs, private companies, social partners, and social enterprises. Projects must be addressed to specific target groups and achieve the aims set by the Ministry of Economic Development (the Managing Authority for ESF). Since 2015, ESF support addressed to individual persons is implemented mostly at the regional level and managed by regional authorities with the Ministry of Economic Development playing a coordinating role.

Overview of vocational education and training policies

Vocational education and training (VET) has a long tradition in Poland. Before 1989, it was the main type of secondary education. However, in many cases, the quality of this education was considered unsatisfactory. In the 1990s, alongside the collapse of many industrial enterprises and the development of other sectors of the economy, the popularity of vocational education declined and increasing numbers of youth began to choose general secondary education. Additionally, VET did not receive heavy investment, further intensifying the challenges faced by the sector.

Recent years have seen a slow revival of vocational education with increasing participation in VET as a secondary education option. The importance of VET has also been emphasised by Polish authorities in many documents and strategies. This change is mostly due to the decreasing advantage (in terms of wages and the probability of finding a job) of general and higher education, especially poor quality higher education; and the shortage of well-educated technicians and skilled workers in some sectors of the economy.

For the past several years, the Polish government has designated vocational education and training as one of its priorities for educational policy and labour market policy. The Ministry of National Education and the Ministry of Family, Labour and Social Policy underline the importance of increasing the quality of VET, its attractiveness to students, and better matching it to the needs of the labour market. The Ministry of Economic Development also supports this approach.

In 2013, the Government approved a document entitled *The Prospect of Learning Throughout Life*, prepared jointly by all interested parties, described in more detail in the textbox below.

Box 1.1. **Strategic perspective of VET**

In 2013, the Polish government approved a strategic document, titled *The Prospect of Learning Throughout Life*, prepared by a team consisting of representatives of the Ministry of National Education, Ministry of Labour and Social Policy, Ministry of Regional Development, Ministry of Economy, (now combined into the Ministry of Economic Development) and other key actors. This strategic document lists key areas of development in vocational education and training, with a special focus on matching VET to the needs of the labour market. The most important areas are listed below:

- Improvement of the education of key VET competences;
- Improvement of the attractiveness and flexibility of VET – development of flexible forms and improvement of the content of VET, enabling flexible mobility between different forms of VET, including vocational schools in the system of adult education, improvements in publicising vocational education, and developing mechanisms of quality assurance in VET;
- Reinforcing the involvement of employers in VET, with particular emphasis on improving practical training, adapting the content of education and training to employers' expectations, and creating sectoral centres of vocational and continuous learning;
- Development of work-based VET;
- Improving the competences of teachers working in VET;
- Development of mechanisms to validate the effects of learning; and
- Development of lifelong educational and vocational guidance.

The system of VET, and especially initial VET, is regulated by the Law on the Education System. The entire system is managed by the Ministry of National Education, which specifies a number of critical education issues for the system, such as: forms of learning, including forms of practical vocational learning; expected results of learning; external vocational exams; requirements for teachers, including their preparation and continuing education and mechanisms of professional promotion; and mechanisms and forms of the pedagogic supervision of schools.

In Poland, there are several VET schemes, enabling flexible movements between different levels of education. These are described in more detail below.

Initial vocational education and training (IVET)

Upper secondary (general and vocational) education starts at the age of 16. It lasts 2-4 years depending on the type of school, and most vocational students complete their IVET at the age of 19-20. There are three types of IVET schools:

- Technical upper secondary school – the education lasts four years, after which students can proceed to take vocational exams, as well as the general upper secondary school education exam (matura), which, if passed, provides entry into university.
- Basic vocational school – the education lasts three years and students proceed to take the vocational exam. An education in this type of school does not enable a pupil to take the general upper secondary education exam (matura).
- Supplementary technical upper secondary school – the education last two years, and is offered to graduates of basic vocational schools.

Another important type of initial VET is the apprenticeship scheme. This type of IVET, accessible to students at the age of at least 16, combines vocational education in the work place – usually a craft trade – with theoretical education, where the student acquires general education and the theoretical preparation for the occupation. The latter type of education may be provided in basic vocational school (for the vast majority of students) or in courses. Table 1 presents the number of students in different types of IVET.

Table 1.1. **Number of students in different types of IVET (0-18 years old), Poland, 2014**

Type of school	Number of students
Basic vocational schools	184 454
Technical upper secondary schools	515 172
Apprenticeships in craft trades	73 575

Source: CSO (2014), *Education in 2013/2014 school year*, Warsaw; MLSAPC, *Information on education 2014*, *www.zrp.pl/Dzia%C5%82alno%C5%9B%C4%87ZRP/O%C5%9Bwiatazawodowa/Egzaminy/Raportyzwynik%C3%B3wdzia%C5%82alno%C5%9Bcio%C5%9Bwiatowej/tabid/393/language/pl-PL/Default.aspx.*

Students who have completed upper secondary school (general or technical) are allowed to enter a post-secondary vocational school. In some cases, the general upper secondary education certificate (matura) is required. The education lasts usually two and a half years. Post-secondary schools are divided into vocational schools, colleges of social work, and teacher training institutions (foreign language teacher training colleges and teacher training colleges). Post-secondary schools are also divided into schools for youth, special schools, and schools for adults.

VET for adults

VET for adults is an area mainly regulated by two ministries: the Ministry of National Education is responsible for the vocational education of adults for the occupations listed in the classification of occupations for education (about 200 occupations); and the Ministry of Family, Labour and Social Policy is responsible for other forms of training and courses for adults. There are also other ministries involved in vocational education and training of adults (e.g. Ministry of Economic Development).

VET for adults in occupations listed in the classification of occupations for education

A reform of the vocational education system was implemented in 2012. One key objective of the reform was to establish a more flexible system of VET education for adults. Before the reform, vocational schools (basic and secondary) existed for adults in Poland. The main weakness of these schools was the long duration of adult education, discouraging many from participating. Thus, the reform introduced a new, shorter form of learning – vocational qualification courses. Vocational qualification courses can be full-time (learning activities taking place at least three times a week) or part-time (learning activities take place at least once every two weeks for two days). Except for practical and laboratory training, which has to be organised in a traditional way, the methods and techniques of distance education can be used. Vocational qualification courses can be offered by:

- Centres of vocational and continuing education (offering vocational education for youth and for adults),
- Centres of continuing education (offering vocational education for adults),
- Centres of practical education (offering practical vocational education for youth and vocational education for adults),
- Vocational training institutions (offering vocational qualification courses and other vocational courses for adults).

The classification of occupations was recently changed in 2012 Although the classification is not closed, the introduction of a new occupation is usually a lengthy process (taking at least a year); thus, adapting a qualification to the changing situation on the labour market is rather slow. However, during panel discussions for this OECD study, participants recalled examples of new, successful occupations introduced recently. In 2015, three new occupations were launched. In forthcoming years, the Ministry of National Education plans a complex review of the classification in close co-operation with social partners to make it more consistent with the needs of the labour market.

The Ministry of National Education also prepared a list of qualifications for each occupation. One occupation may consist of several qualifications, which should make the education system more flexible and accessible. Each qualification is an independent, complete whole that feature learning competences such as specific knowledge, skills and personal and social competence. These are described as learning outcomes in the core curriculum and may be separately confirmed in the system of national vocational exams. As a result, most of the skills can be taught as qualifying vocational courses (LCO) in the system of lifelong learning for adults.

Other forms of training and courses for adults

Private institutions, non-governmental organisations, as well as public institutions offer a very broad scope of training and courses in vocational education, general education, personal development, etc. Some of them are regulated by law (e.g. driving licences), others are regulated by sector boards (e.g. qualifications standards for the banking sector, developed by the Association of Polish Banks), or based on international standards (e.g. the European Computer Driving Licence).

These programmes and courses may be subsidised or financed from public sources, e.g. the European Social Fund or the National Training Fund (managed by poviat labour offices). The main institution responsible for this area of public policy is the Polish Agency of Enterprise Development (supervised by the Ministry of Economic Development and the Ministry of Family, Labour and Social Policy).

Recently, public authorities have made the effort to regulate the market in order to ensure better quality training (at least the training financed by public sources). To do so, a new mechanism has been recently introduced: the Register of Development Services, managed by the Polish Agency of Enterprise Development. Each provider of training or courses, who would like to provide skills development services, should fulfil criteria and register in the Register.

While the register does not include all institutions, a number of conclusions can be drawn from analysing the providers on the register. Around 95% of these institutions are private, and almost 55% represent an individual person who has registered as a business entity. There is a large variety of companies, NGOs, educational institutions and private persons that provide training and education, although in many cases, the quality of training is not considered to be satisfactory.

Other mechanisms of quality assurance are the Polish Qualifications Framework (PQF) and the closely related Register of Qualifications. In order to be registered and referenced to the PQF, each qualification must meet quality requirements. The new system is still under construction and is not fully functional yet.

Overview of economic development policy

Economic development policy is managed by the Ministry of Economic Development; however, a number of actors are involved. The most important fields of activities are support for small and medium enterprises, special economic areas, support for research and development and innovation, promotion of Polish enterprises and the support of exports.

There are a number of instruments and institutions that support economic development and act at the national, regional and local levels. Many of them are interconnected and co-operate with each other. Support for economic development is financed mostly by European funds. Thus, most of the actors operate within the framework of operational programmes, financed by the European Regional Development Fund or the European Social Fund.

At the national level, the most important actors are the Polish Enterprise Development Agency and the National Centre for Research and Development. The Polish Enterprise Development Agency (PAED) is a central agency, supervised by the Ministry of Economic Development and Ministry of Family, Labour and Social Policy. The Agency supports mostly small and medium enterprises and focusses on areas such as innovation and e-business.

Another important governmental agency is the National Centre for Research and Development, supervised by the Ministry of Science and Higher Education. The Centre carries out programmes that support innovation, research and development, as well as the implementation of innovative solutions both at research institutions and enterprises. The Centre especially focuses on co-operation between scientific entities and enterprises.

Programmes are financed from both national and European funds. Support for enterprises, especially industrial ones, is also provided by the Industrial Development Agency.

At the regional level, the most important actor is the regional government (voivodeship). It can act directly or through specialised agencies. The most important regional instrument for economic development is the regional operational programme, financed by European funds and managed by regional authorities. The new wave of programmes covers the period of 2014-23. The programmes include direct support for small and medium enterprises (in the form of grants, loans, services), as well as investments in business development (investment areas, institutions supporting business, co-operation between businesses and research units, and the development of business clusters).

In Poland, there are also about 60 regional development agencies. Most of them were established in the 1990s as instruments supporting local and regional economic development, with the support of development aid from foreign sources. Agencies usually act in the form of a company, owned or co-owned by regional and local authorities, enterprises or associations of employers, or the Industrial Development Agency.

After 2004, many agencies in Poland became part of the system of European Fund implementers that provide support to enterprises. Currently, many of them implement projects addressed to new or existing enterprises, providing funds (grants for start-ups, loans for existing enterprises), and services to business. The agencies also support innovation in enterprises (providing grants, support, and enabling contacts between actors). Some of them also invest in infrastructure for business, establishing technology parks and business incubators. In some cases, agencies implement projects related to the labour market, including supporting start-ups, providing training for employees and employers, or supporting non-governmental organisations.

At the regional and local levels, technology parks are important incentives for economic development. These institutions usually operate as companies and provide space, infrastructure and support for enterprise development, especially innovative ones. Although their capacity is growing in terms of the number of companies operating in parks, it is still challenging to attract enterprises which are the most innovative, invest in new technologies, co-operate with research and scientific entities, and implement projects with international partners (PAED, 2012). This shows that technological parks have only partially achieved their goals.

Another important instrument is the Special Economic Zone (SEZ), established primarily to accelerate regional economic growth, utilise greyfield infrastructure and assets, and create new jobs (KPMG, 2014). SEZs were established primarily in areas with significant structural problems (low employment, low level of economic activity) in inhabited areas. The main aim of the SEZ was to attract investors (Polish and foreign) by offering incentives such as tax exemptions and access to infrastructure. Currently 14 SEZs operate in Poland, however their borders are flexible and can be adjusted to the needs of the local economy and interest of investors. In practise, the area of the zones is currently much larger than when they were established, and in many cases, has extended far beyond their original boundaries, often covering two or three provinces. According to analyses, SEZs proved to be an effective instrument supporting economic development and increasing employment. According to estimates at the end of 2012, 1 million PLN of state aid for enterprises operation in SEZs generated 6,95 million PLN of investments generated by those enterprises, 4,5 million in taxes paid by those enterprises, 31 jobs in enterprises operating in SEZs, including 17 new job positions (Pastusiak et al., 2012).

Note

1. One explanatory factor may be that unemployed people must register at poviat labour offices in order to receive health care coverage for themselves and their families. This can lead to situations where people not actually looking for work or already working informally register without having real intentions to look for work. See OECD (2014a) for more information.

References

Andrews, D., A. Caldera Sánchez and Å. Johansson (2011), "Towards a Better Understanding of the Informal Economy", *OECD Economics Department Working Papers*, No. 873, OECD Publishing, Paris, *http://dx.doi.org/10.1787/5kgb1mf88x28-en.*

CSO (2014), *Oświata i wychowanie w roku szkolnym 2013/2014, (Education in 2013/2014 school year)*, Central Statistical Office, Warsaw.

KPMG (2014), *20 years of Special Economic Zones in Poland A Guide to SEZs, www.kpmg.com/PL/en/IssuesAndInsights/ArticlesPublications/Documents/A-Guide-to-Special-Economic-Zones-in-Poland.pdf.*

MLSPAPC (2015), *Informacja oświatowa 2014,* [Information on education, 2014], Association of Professional Crafts, *www.zrp.pl.*

MLSP (2014), *Profilowanie pomocy dla osób bezrobotnych; Podręcznik dla pracowników powiatowych urzędów pracy* [Profiling support for the unemployed; Manual for employees of poviat labour offices], Ministry of Labour and Social Policy, Warsaw.

MLSP (2008), *Analiza funkcjonowania urzędów pracy po ich włączeniu do administracji samorządowej* [Analysis of the functioning of labour offices after their incorporation to local government], Ministry of Labour and Social Policy, Warsaw.

OECD (2016a), *OECD Economic Surveys: Poland 2016*, OECD Publishing, Paris, *http://dx.doi.org/10.1787/eco_surveys-pol-2016-en.*

OECD (2016b), *Employment rate* (indicator), *http://dx.doi.org/10.1787/1de68a9b-en* (accessed on 29 March 2016).

OECD (2016c), *Unemployment rate* (indicator), *http://dx.doi.org/10.1787/997c8750-en* (accessed on 29 March 2016).

OECD (2016d), *Labour force participation rate* (indicator), *http://dx.doi.org/10.1787/8a801325-en* (accessed on 30 March 2016).

OECD (2016e), *Youth unemployment rate* (indicator), *http://dx.doi.org/10.1787/c3634df7-en* (accessed on 30 March 2016).

OECD (2016f), "OECD Regional Labour Statistics", *OECD Regional Statistics* (database), *http://dx.doi.org/10.1787/region-data-en* (accessed on 29 February 2016).

OECD (2015), *Education at a Glance 2015: OECD Indicators*, OECD Publishing, Paris, *http://dx.doi.org/10.1787/eag-2015-en.*

OECD (2014a), *OECD Economic Surveys: Poland 2014*, OECD Publishing, Paris, *http://dx.doi.org/10.1787/eco_surveys-pol-2014-en.*

OECD (2014b), "Aggregate National Accounts: Gross domestic product", *OECD National Accounts Statistics* (database), *http://dx.doi.org/10.1787/data-00001-en.*

OECD (2014c), "Labour Force Statistics: Employment by activities and status", *OECD Employment and Labour Market Statistics* (database), *http://dx.doi.org/10.1787/data-00289-en.*

OECD (2013), *OECD Skills Outlook 2013: First Results from the Survey of Adult Skills*, OECD Publishing, Paris, *http://dx.doi.org/10.1787/9789264204256-en.*

PAED (2012), *Benchmarking of technology parks in Poland; 2012 edition*, Polish Agency for Enterprise Development, Warsaw, *www.pi.gov.pl/eng/chapter_86520.asp.*

Pastusiak, R., J. Gajdka, M. Jabłońska, J. Keller, J. Koziński and B. Krzeczewski (2013), *Ocena efektywności funkcjonowania specjalnych stref ekonomicznych w Polsce [Evaluation of effectiveness of the special economic zones]* , University of Lodz, Faculty of Economics and Sociology; Lodz, *www.mg.gov.pl/Wspieranie+przedsiebiorczosci/Wsparcie+finansowe+i+inwestycje/Specjalne+strefy+ekonomiczne/Efekty+SSE.*

Chapter 2

Overview of the Polish case study areas

To better understand the role of the local level in contributing to job creation and productivity, this OECD review examined local activities in two Polish sub-regions: the city of Poznań and the Radomski sub-region. This chapter provides a labour market and economic overview of each region as well as the results from an OECD LEED statistical tool which looks at the relationship between skills supply and demand at the sub-regional level.

Overview of the Poznań and Radomski sub-regions

In-depth fieldwork for this study was undertaken in two sub-regions in Poland: the city of Poznań and the Radomski sub-region. These two areas were selected after consultation between the OECD and the government, based on their contrasting economic and labour market characteristics. The sub-region category in Poland falls between the voivodeship (regional) and poviat (county) level. It is used only for statistical purposes and usually does not correspond to administrative units.

The Poznań sub-region is in the western part of Poland, and strictly corresponds to the administrative borders of the city of Poznań, thus containing only one local authority. It is a capital of the Wielkopolska province, as well as one of Poland's largest cities. This sub-region is populated by 550 000 people. While the sub-region corresponds only to the urban area comprised of the city of Poznań, its functional economic area also includes the surrounding municipalities in the area around the city of Poznań, which themselves form the Poznański sub-region. Although the analysis focussed on the city of Poznań, the Poznański sub-region is also taken into consideration in many cases, as both together make up a local travel-to-work area.

Poznań lies between the capitals of two neighbouring countries: Warsaw and Berlin. It is thus one of the main logistical centres in Poland and plays an important part in the trade flow between western and eastern Europe.

The Radomski sub-region is part of Mazowsze, the largest voivodeship in Poland. The Radomski sub-region has 620 000 people. The Radomski sub-region includes both rural and urban areas, with about half of its population living in urban areas. The main city of the sub-region is Radom, with 217 000 residents. The sub-region also contains 6 other municipalities (gmina) with their own local governments.

The sub-region is located about 100 km south of Warsaw, the capital of Poland, where most of Poland's economic activities are concentrated. The economic and labour market situation in Radom has been rather difficult for many years, especially in comparison to the situation in Warsaw. Radom and the neighbouring poviats, with a traditional industrial economy, were heavily impacted by the transformation process and collapse of the industrial economy.

Local labour market

There is a significant difference between the two sub-regions. Poznań has one of the better performing local labour markets, with an unemployment rate significantly below the Polish average, while the unemployment rate in the Radomski sub-region is one of the highest in Poland.

The structure of unemployment also differs. In the Radomski sub-region, the probability of leaving the ranks of the unemployed is significantly lower than in Poznań: in 2014, the share of long-term unemployed persons among all the unemployed was 51% in the Radomski sub-region and 36% in Poznań.

Figure 2.1. **Registered unemployment rate, the Radomski and Poznań sub-regions in comparison to Poland, 2004-14**

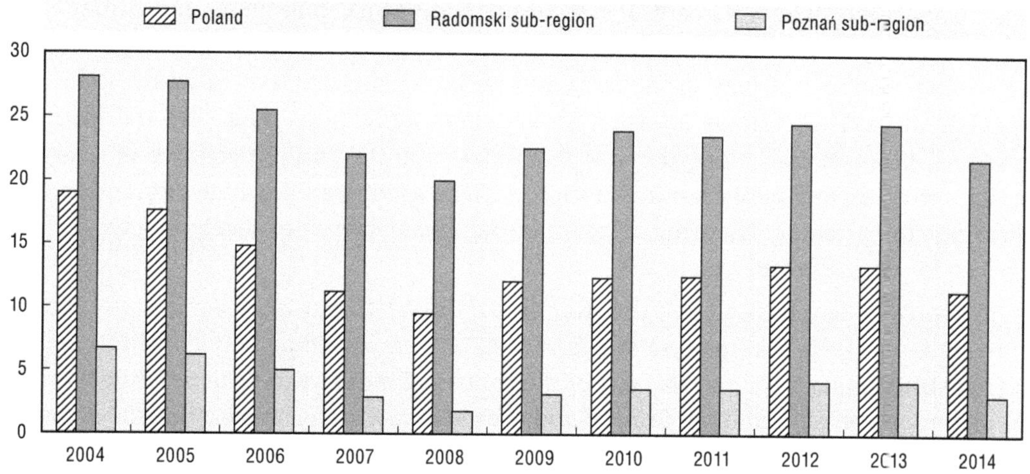

Source: Central Statistical Office, Local Data Bank, *https://bdl.stat.gov.pl/BDL/dane/temat.*

Looking below the sub-regional level, the situation within the Radomski sub-region is varied. It contains the Szydłowiecki county (poviat), with highest unemployment rate in Poland as well as the Białobrzeski county, with an unemployment rate 20 percentage points lower than in the Szydłowiecki county (however still higher than the average for Poland).

Figure 2.2. **Registered unemployment rate by poviat in the Radomski sub-region, 2014**

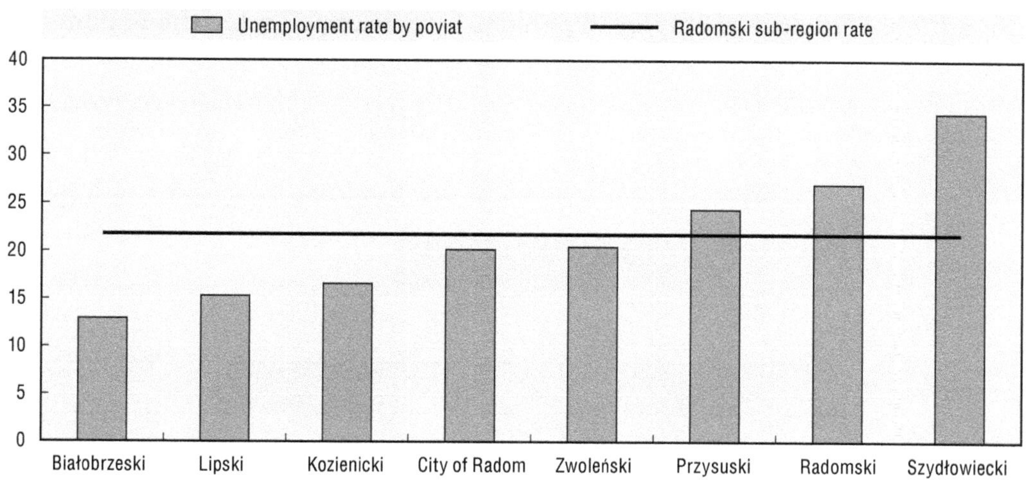

Source: Central Statistical Office, Local Data Bank, *https://bdl.stat.gov.pl/BDL/dane/temat.*

The recent economic crisis impacted both sub-regions (with an increase in unemployment and a slowdown of economic growth), but did not significantly change the situation of both labour markets. As discussed in Chapter 1, Poland managed to emerge from the crisis without experiencing a severe economic recession and without serious impact to the labour market. In Poznań, for example, the number of employed persons between 2008 and 2013 increased by 1%.

The structure of the economy and employment of both sub-regions also differ significantly. The structure of employment in Poznań is typical of urban areas, with almost

80% of employment in services, with considerable diversity in the types of jobs available (public and private sectors; high- and low-skilled; larger, international enterprises and local businesses). Twenty percent of employed people work in industry and construction. The structure of the economy in Poznań has been changing in recent years, with decreasing numbers of jobs in industry and an increasing number of white collar jobs, especially in such sectors as information and communications, financial and insurance activities, professional, scientific and technical activities, administrative and support service activities, and public administration, with an accompanying high demand for well-educated professionals. There are at least two branches of services developing very rapidly: services for business and logistics.

It should be emphasised that the structure of the Polish economy significantly changed in the 1990s. In 1988, according to the census, 42% of employed person worked in industry and construction, and Poznań was one of the centres of industry in Poland. While Poznań is still an important industrial centre in Poland, jobs in industry have moved outside of the city. Between 2005 and 2013, the number of persons employed in industry and construction in Poznań declined by almost 20%, while in the same period, the number of employed persons in industry and construction increased by 17% in the Poznański sub-region (districts surrounding the city of Poznań), accounting for over 40% of all persons in employment. This clearly shows the importance of considering Poznań and the surrounding sub-region in tandem because of their strong economic and social connections. However, their labour markets differ significantly: Poznań has become a centre of professional services, while the most important economic sectors for employment in the surrounding districts are industry, construction, trade, storage, and agriculture.

Figure 2.3. **Structure of employed persons by economic sector, the Radomski and Poznań sub-regions in comparison to Poland, 2013**

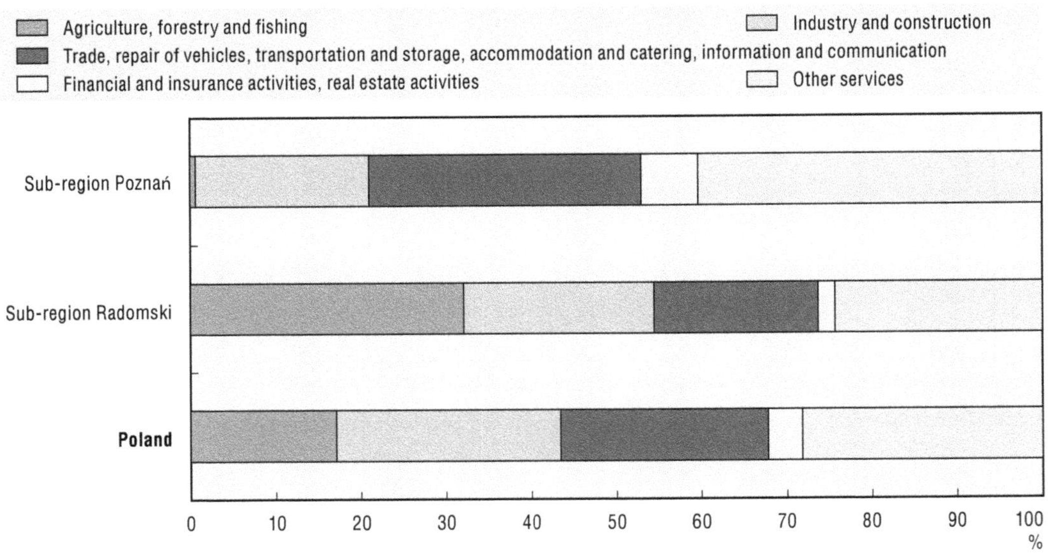

Source: Central Statistical Office, Local Data Bank, *https://bdl.stat.gov.pl/BDL/dane/temat.*

The structure of the economy and labour market in the Radomski sub-region is more typical of urban-rural areas. In less developed areas, there is a very high share of employment in agriculture. One third of employment is in the agricultural sector, which is almost twice the national average, while there is a relatively small share of employment in the service sector. The economic transformation during the 1990s caused a significant reduction of employment, many closures of industrial enterprises and the rapid growth of unemployment, which continues to persist. Unlike in Poznań, the service sector was unable to absorb as many people who lost their jobs. The city of Radom is the most important centre of the sub-region, in terms of the economy and labour market. Thus, the fall of industry in Radom also impacted the other cities in the Radomski sub-region.

However, recent years have brought about a slow economic rebirth of the sub-region. The fastest developing sector of economy, in terms of the number of employed, are services (trade, vehicle repairs, storage, accommodations and catering, information and communications). Between 2005 and 2013, the number of employed people in services increased by 27%. However, this sector has a sizeable share of low quality jobs, which are low-paid, often temporary, and characterised by non-standard work contracts.

At the same time, the number of employed persons in industry and construction increased by 8%. Industrial enterprises concentrate in Radom, but they are also located in Kozienice (the site of one of the most innovative power stations) and the Radomski poviat (surrounding Radom).

Education levels

The two sub-regions selected for in-depth analyses differ significantly in terms of the level of education. The most detailed data comes from the latest census (2011). In Poznań, 30% of the population aged 13 and older has completed tertiary education while in the Radomski sub-region, only 15% of the population achieved such a level of education. The Radomski sub-region has a much larger share of its population with the lowest level of education – primary and lower secondary.

The structure of education in the Radomski sub-region is influenced by the situation in rural areas, which is usually worse than in urban areas. However, the differences are also substantial between the cities of Radom and Poznań, which are both relatively urban areas.

Figure 2.4. **Highest level of education achieved for the population aged 13 and over, the Radomski and Poznań sub-regions in comparison to Poland, 2011**

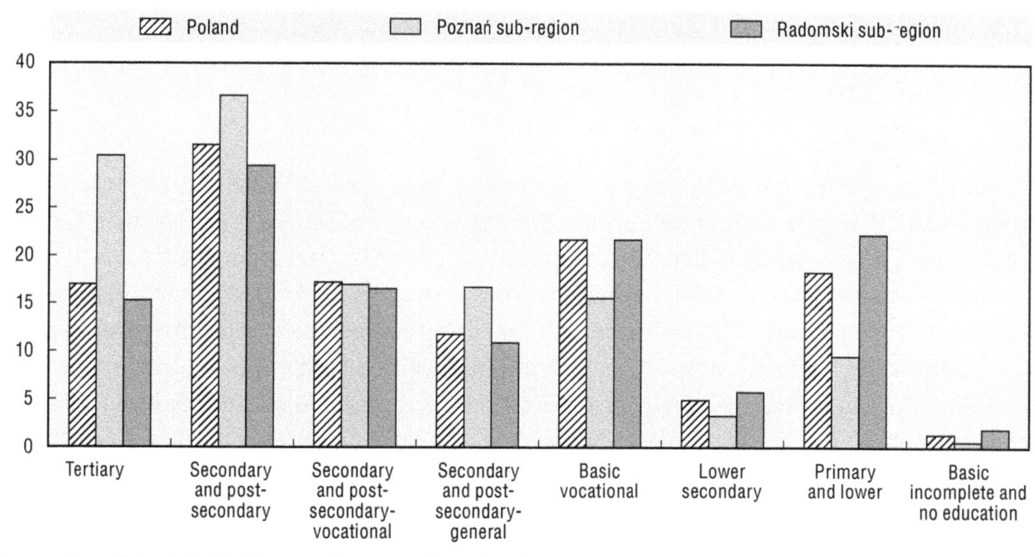

Source: Central Statistical Office, Local Data Bank, National Census 2011, *https://bdl.stat.gov.pl/BDL/dane/temat.*

Commuting patterns

In 2011, the Central Statistical Office conducted an in-depth analysis of commuting patterns and travel to work areas on the basis of National Census. The mobility patterns differ between Poznań and the Radomski sub-region. Radom is a centre for the sub-regional labour market, with approximately 80 000 jobs, which is the second highest number in the Mazowiecki Region (Warsaw is in first place with 1.28 million jobs). In Radom itself, there are 1 250 active persons for every 1 000 jobs, which indicates a mismatch in the local labour market where the supply of labour is higher than the demand, causing a high unemployment rate. In other counties of the sub-region, the situation is similar or even worse (MORP, 2013).

In 2011, an average of 8 000 people travelled to work to Radom every day, and 6 500 people travelled from Radom to other cities (a ratio of 1.2:1). Among those travelling to Radom, 66% live in Radomski County, which surrounds Radom. The second source of those travelling to Radom was Szydłowiecki County (but it only accounts for about 6% of all persons travelling to Radom). Among those travelling *from* Radom, 47% travel to Warsaw, which has the largest labour market in Poland, and a further 23% travel to Radomski County surrounding Radom.

The situation is different in Poznań. In recent years, Poznań has experienced negative migration – a significant number of people moved to surrounding communities (suburbanisation of the city), while still working in Poznań. According to the census, the scale of the daily migration in Poznań is much larger than in Radom. About 85 000 people travel every day to Poznań, while 24 000 people travel from Poznań. The relationship between these two values is 3.5 (1.2 for Radom). Around 37% of the people travelling to Poznań live in Poznański County (surrounding Poznań), while a further 48% travel from other counties of the Wielkopolska Region. This data, although based on administrative sources (which in this case are not always accurate), show that Poznań is an attractive place to work for many people and its administrative boundaries do not fit the travel to work area. However, local authorities in Poznań, aware of this phenomenon, created the Observatory of the Labour Market for the Poznań Agglomeration, which provides data and conducts research on Poznań and a number of neighbouring communities. The area of the agglomeration is much closer to the travel to work area and allows for more accurate analyses and studies.

Employment, training and education services in the case study areas

Employment services

As employment services operate under the same law in both sub-regions, their structure and tasks are similar. In Poznań, there is one poviat labour office, serving the City of Poznań and the Poznański district (surrounding Poznań). In December 2014, almost 16 000 unemployed persons were registered with the office (two-thirds from Poznań and one-third from the Poznański district). The poviat labour office co-operates with non-governmental organisations in providing support for the unemployed, supporting social enterprises, or running social integration centres. An important partner is the Municipal Centre for Family Assistance, which provides social assistance services – although the scope of services differs, in many cases, the Centre provides services for the unemployed and coordinates its activities with the poviat labour office. The Centre has one headquarter and six branches. Likewise in the Poznański district, each county has a social assistance centre. The regional labour office is also located in Poznań, but it provides a limited scope of services for individual persons.

A number of private institutions providing recruitment and training services also operate in Poznań. There are 415 registered employment agencies and almost 500 training institutions. Registers, managed by Ministry of Family, Labour and Social Policy, do not provide information on the number of persons served by those institutions.

In the Radomski sub-region, there are seven poviat labour offices covering eight districts (the poviat labour office in Radom covers both Radom and the Radomski district surrounding Radom). The largest poviat labour office is located in Radom. In December 2014, over 33 000 persons were registered as unemployed. Two other important poviat labour offices are in Szydłowiec and Przysucha – in both about 5 000 people were registered. A local branch of the voluntary labour corps is also located in Radom (providing employment and education services for youth at risk of social exclusion).

Radom also has a number of private employment agencies (38) and training institutions (84) that provide services to individuals and employers. Their numbers are significantly lower than in Poznań.

Education

Poznań and Radom also differ in terms of the presence of academic institutions. About 28 higher education institutions operate in Poznań, some of them acknowledged as among the best in Poland (Adam Mickiewicz University in Poznań, Poznań University of Economics, Poznań University of Life Sciences). As in other parts of Poland, there are also a number of higher education institutions operating in Poznań, often private, although they often provide poor quality education. In the Radomski sub-region, there are nine higher education institutions. The most important one is the Kazimierz Pulaski University of Technology and Humanities, formerly the Kazimierz Pulaski Radom Polytechnic.

The difference between the Radomski sub-region and Poznań is even more visible in terms of the number of students. In 2014, there were almost 117 000 students in Poznań, while in Radom there were 10 500. Moreover, the number of students has been steadily decreasing during recent years. Between 2004 and 2014, the number of students in Radom decreased by 60%, while there was a much more modest decrease of 8% Poznań. This is a result of two processes: demographic – (decreasing numbers of youth), as well as economic

Figure 2.5. **Number of students, Radomski and Poznań sub-regions, 2004-14**

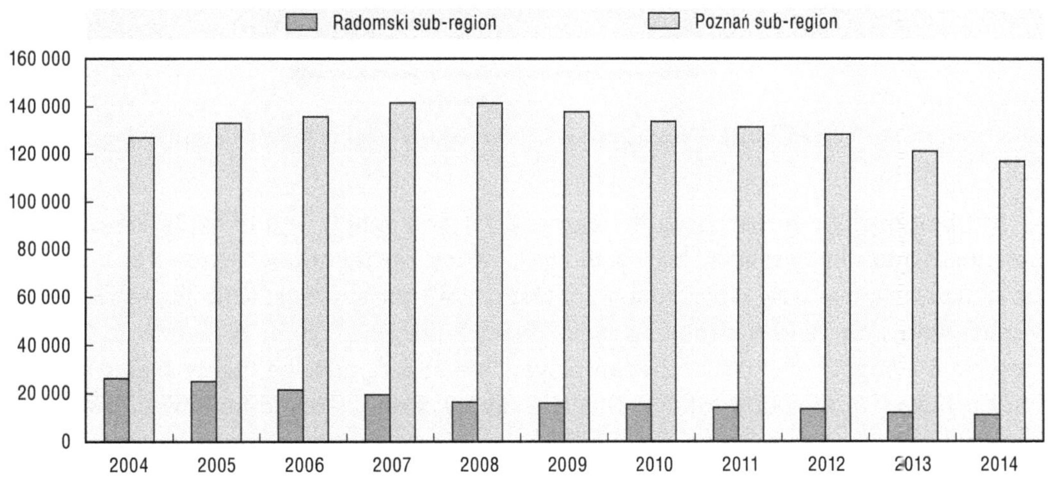

Source: Central Statistical Office, Local Data Bank, *https://bdl.stat.gov.pl/BDL/dane/temat.*

(increasing access to better higher education institutions offering better quality education, which are usually located in larger cities such as Warsaw, Poznań, and Kraków). Thus Poznań attracts many students not only from the Wielkopolska province, but also from other provinces. In the case of Radom, youth often decide to migrate to other cities to study.

Access to secondary education is similar in both sub-regions. Although the structure of the schools relies on decisions of the local government, it is more or less adjusted to the number of students.

Balance between skills supply and demand at the sub-national level

The LEED Programme has developed a statistical tool to understand the relationship between skills supply and demand within local labour markets (Froy, Giguère and Meghnagi, 2012). This tool can help to provide policy makers with an understanding of sub-national distribution of skills supply and demand. This, in turn, can inform the development of place-based policy approaches at the local level based on specific challenges and opportunities related to skills.

Figure 2.6. **Understanding the relationship between skills supply and demand**

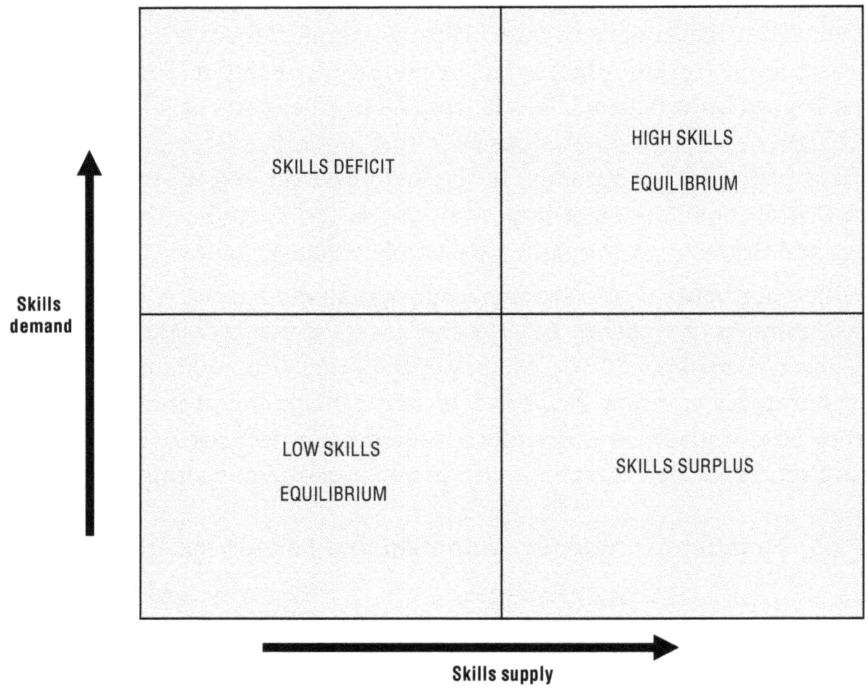

Source: Froy, F. and S. Giguère (2010), "Putting in Place Jobs that Last: A Guide to Rebuilding Quality Employment at Local Level".

In the top-right corner, both the demand for and supply and of skills are relatively high, a situation known as a "high skill equilibrium". In the top-left corner of the figure above, there is a relatively high demand for skills, while the supply of skills is relatively low – in other words, there may be skills deficits. In such places, it can be beneficial to focus on boosting the supply of skills so that employers are able to find the highly skilled workers that they need. In the bottom-left corner the supply of and demand for low skills are both relatively low, creating a "low skills trap". The challenge facing policymakers is to get the economy moving towards the top-right corner. Lastly, in the bottom-right corner, a relatively low demand for skills is met by a relatively high supply of skills, suggesting a

Box 2.1. **Explaining the diagnostic tool**

The analysis is carried out at Territorial Level 3 regions (regions with populations ranging between 150 000-800 000). The supply of skills was measured by the percentage of the population with post-secondary education. The demand for skills was approximated using a composite index: percentage of the population employed in medium-high skilled occupations and GVA per worker (weighted at .25 and .75 respectively). The indices are standardised using the inter-decile method and are compared with the national median. Further explanations on the methodology can be found in Froy, Giguère and Meghnagi, 2012.

Source: Froy, F., S. Giguère and M. Meghnagi (2012), "Skills for Competitiveness: A Synthesis Report".

need to focus on working with employers to better utilise the skills the local workforce has to offer, either through higher value added production or improved work organisation.

This typology was applied to Polish TL3 regions, including the local case study areas of the Poznań and Radomski sub-regions – see Figure 2.7a.

Figure 2.7a. **Skills supply and demand: Sub-regions in Poland, chart, 2011**

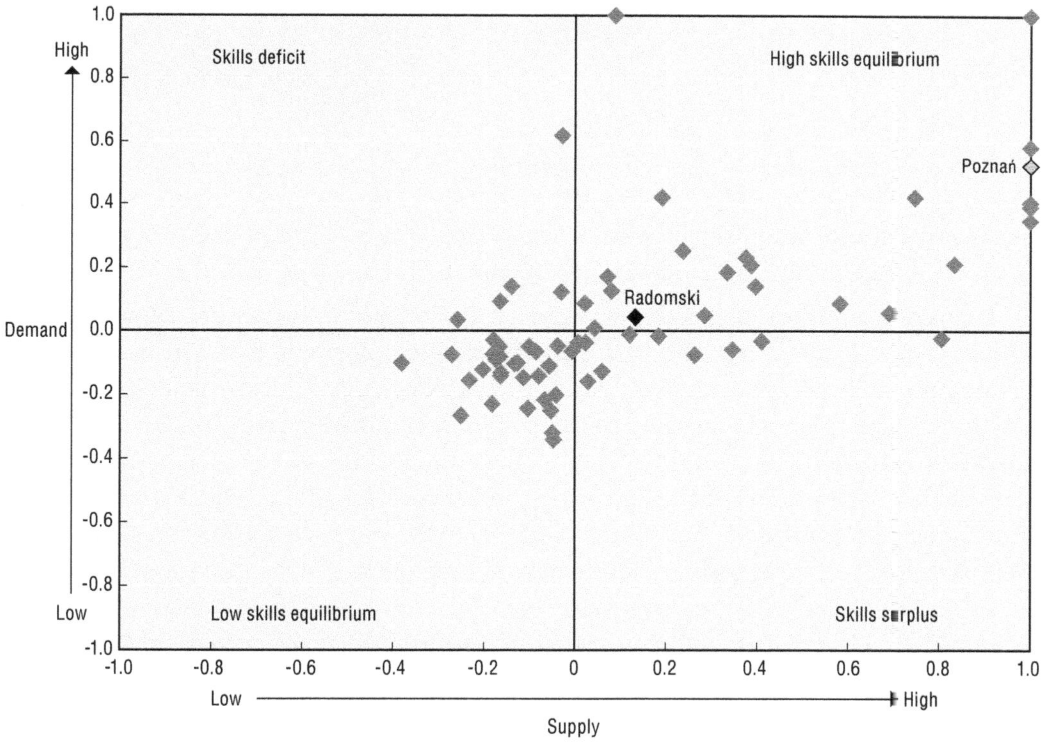

Twenty-three of Poland's sub-regions can be considered to be in a "high skills equilibrium", while 28 fall into a "low skills equilibrium". Ten fall into the "skills surplus" quadrant, and finally, five are considered to be in a "skill deficit". Both case study areas fall into a high skills equilibrium, although in the Radomski sub-region, skills demand is only marginally above the median and therefore close to the skills surplus quadrant.

Using the OECD regional typology classifications, one can see that 42% of urban regions and 50% of intermediate regions are in high skills equilibriums. This includes both

Figure 2.7b. **Skills supply and demand: Sub-regions in Poland, map, 2011**

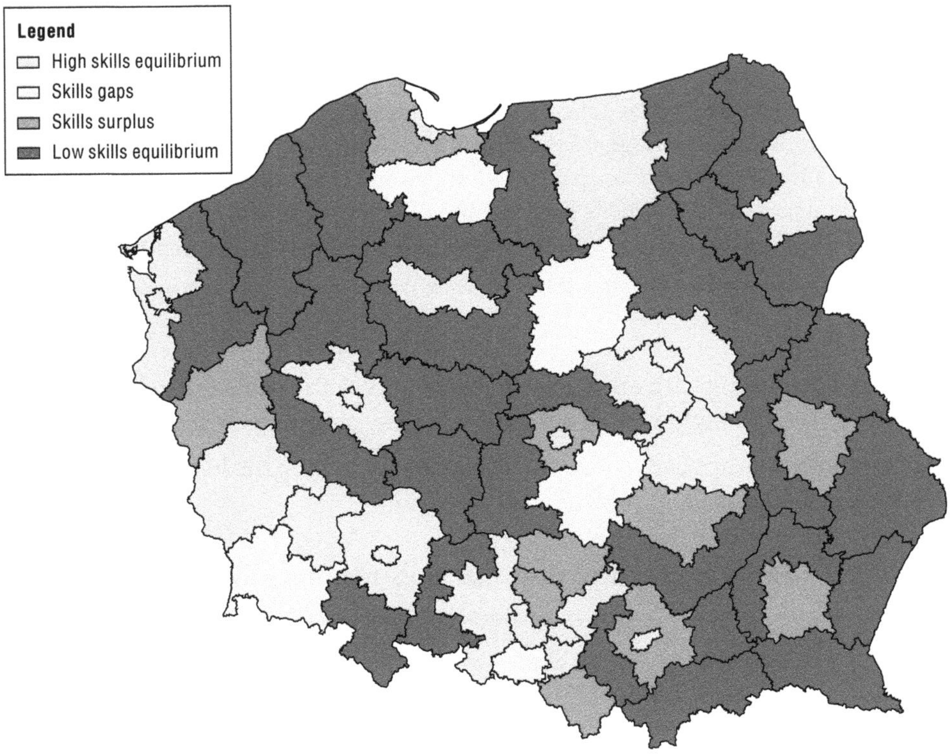

Source: OECD calculations based data from Central Statistical Office, Local Data Bank, *https://bdl.stat.gov.pl/BDL/dane/temat*.

Poznań (urban) and Radomski (intermediate). In contrast, only 24% of rural regions fall into a high skills equilibrium, and over half (56%) fall into low skills equilibrium.

High skill equilibrium sub-regions perform strongest in terms of GDP growth, but perform relatively worse in terms of the registered unemployment rate. This suggests that ensuring an inclusive labour market is a particular challenge for these sub-regions. Skills surplus sub-regions also show comparatively high rates of GDP growth, but have the lowest registered unemployment rate. In such places, inclusiveness of the labour market is relatively less of a priority than increasing the demand for skills. Low skills equilibrium sub-regions perform the worst in terms of GDP growth, and have above average registered unemployment rates, suggesting that the labour market challenges these sub-regions face

Table 2.1. **Overlaying skills supply and demand with other local indicators**

Average for sub-regions falling into each quadrant

	Percent change in GDP (2011-2012)	Registered unemployment rate (2012)	Net international migration as a share of population (2005-2012)	Net inter-regional migration as a share of population (2005-2012)
High skills equilibrium	4.16	15.0	-0.43	0.35
Radomski	*2.05*	*24.6*	*-0.01*	*-1.82*
Poznań	*5.16*	*4.2*	*-0.37*	*-3.53*
Skills deficit	3.56	14.5	-0.20	-1.06
Skills surplus	3.77	13.6	-0.19	-0.12
Low skills equilibrium	3.33	14.6	-0.21	-0.55

Note: All averages are unweighted sub-regional averages.
Source: OECD calculations based data from Central Statistical Office, Local Data Bank, *https://bdl.stat.gov.pl/BDL/dane/temat*.

are particularly challenging. Likewise, skills deficit sub-regions also show below average GDP growth and above average registered unemployment rates.

Turning to migration patterns, high skills equilibrium sub-regions are able to attract internal migrants (as evidenced by their positive intra-regional net migration rate), but lose the highest share of their population to international migration. All of the other sub-regions also show negative rates of net inter-regional migration during the period analysed, with skills deficit sub-regions losing a particularly large share of its population. However, without detailed information available on the skill level of migrants at the TL3 level, it is impossible to say whether this high rate of migration is a result of or a contributing factor to the deficit.

References

Froy, F. and S. Giguère (2010), "Putting in Place Jobs that Last: A Guide to Rebuilding Quality Employment at Local Level", *OECD Local Economic and Employment Development (LEED) Working Papers*, No. 2010/13, OECD Publishing, *https://dx.doi.org/10.1787/5km7jf7qtk9p-en*.

Froy, F., S. Giguère and M. Meghnagi (2012), "Skills for Competitiveness: A Synthesis Report", *OECD Local Economic and Employment Development (LEED) Working Papers*, No. 2012/09, OECD Publishing, *https://dx.doi.org/10.1787/5k98xwskmvr6-en*.

Central Statistical Office, Local Data Bank, *https://bdl.stat.gov.pl/*.

MORP (2013), *Rynek pracy województwa mazowieckiego – analiza przestrzenna*, Trendy rozwojowe mazowsza nr 12/2013 [The labour market of Mazowieckie voivodship – spatial analysis; Development trends of Mazovia No. 12/2013], The Mazovian Office for Regional Planning, Warsaw.

Chapter 3

Local Job Creation Dashboard findings in Poland

This chapter highlights findings from the Local Job Creation Dashboard in Poland. The findings are discussed through the four thematic areas of the OECD review: 1) better aligning policies and programmes to local economic development; 2) adding value through skills; 3) targeting policy to local employment sectors and investing in quality jobs; and 4) being inclusive.

This section presents the main findings from the in-depth fieldwork undertaken in Poland to look at the implementation of employment and skills policies. In the following section, each of the four priority areas of the OECD review are presented and discussed. The full results of the Local Job Creation Dashboard for Poland are presented in the figure below.

Figure 3.1. **Overview of results from Local Job Creation Dashboard**

Theme 1: Better alignment of policy and programmes to local economic development

Flexibility in the delivery of employment and vocational training policies

Flexibility and accountability of poviat labour offices

The OECD defines flexibility as "the possibility to adjust policy at its various design, implementation and delivery stages to make it better adapted to local contexts, actions carried out by other organisations, strategies being pursued, and challenges and opportunities faced" (Giguère and Froy, 2009). Flexibility refers to the latitude that exists in the management system of the employment system, rather than the flexibility of the

Figure 3.2. **Dashboard results: Better aligning programmes and policies to local economic development**

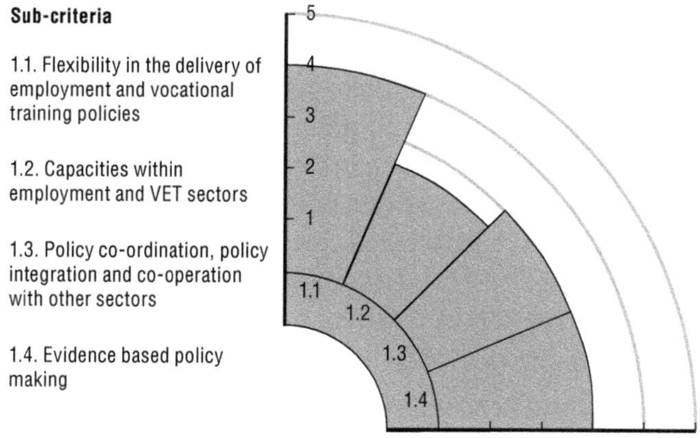

labour market itself. The achievement of local flexibility does not necessarily mean that governments need to politically decentralise (Giguère and Froy, 2009). Rather, flexibility refers to the latitude given to local actors in the areas of designing policies and programmes, managing budgets, setting performance targets, deciding on eligibility, and outsourcing services.

Overall, poviat labour offices (PLOs) have a relatively high level of flexibility compared to other OECD countries. However, when asked in the OECD survey, many still indicated that further flexibility would be beneficial, especially related to programme and strategy design, choice of target groups/eligibility criteria, and budget management. Each of the specific sub-dimensions of flexibility are considered separately for PES below, and the corresponding survey results are shown in the figure below.

Figure 3.3. **Results of OECD survey to poviat labour offices on local flexibility in PES, 2015**

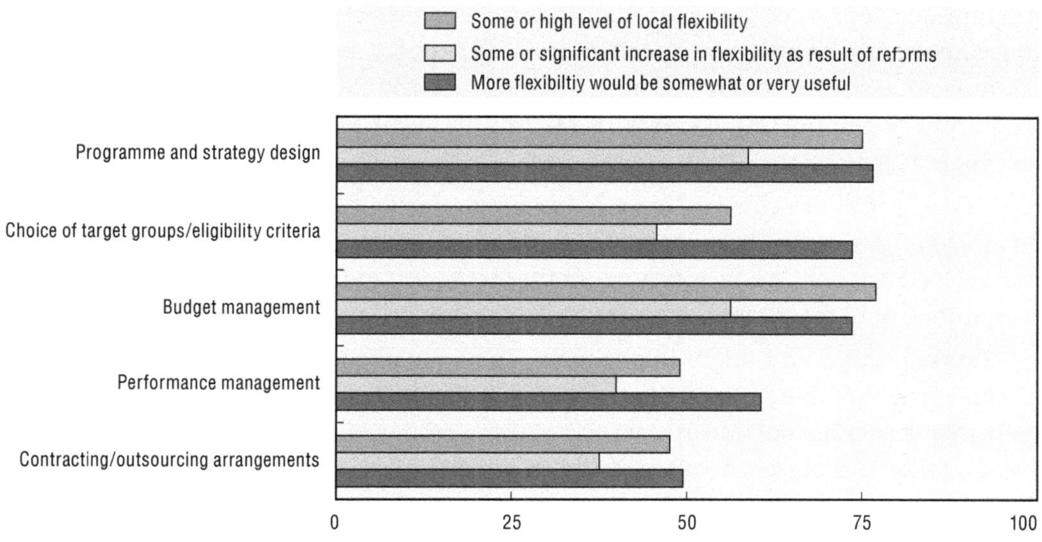

Source: 2015 OECD LEED Survey to poviat labour offices.

Programme and strategy design. In the survey to poviat labour offices, 75% of reported that they had "some" or a high level of flexibility in relation to programme and strategy design, and 59% reported that the recent reforms resulted in "some" or a "significant" increase in flexibility in this area. As discussed in Chapter 1, public employment services were decentralised in Poland in 1999. The main justifications for this shift were to improve the flexibility of PES, as well as to improve co-ordination between PES and other policy fields at the local level (MLSP, 2008). Key actors vary in their opinions regarding the achievement of these objectives. Some of them emphasise that decentralisation has brought positive results, however the level of integration of local labour market policy with other policies is still not sufficient in many cases (MLSP, 2008). Others point out that the achievement of both objectives has been impeded by very detailed national legal regulations that limit the scope of flexibility of poviat labour offices (Coffey, 2012).

Poviat labour offices are allowed to use only those instruments of active labour market policy that are defined in the Law on the Promotion of Employment and Institutions of the Labour Market. The catalogue of available instruments is rather broad, and in the opinion of employment office representatives, is adequate to meet their needs while allowing for flexibility in adjusting to the needs of local labour markets and the unemployed. On the other hand, during interviews, some experts emphasised that such solutions, in practice, reduce incentives for innovative, non-standard actions.

Selecting instruments from the catalogue is a two-fold process. First, poviat labour offices prepare their annual plans, in which they select the instruments they would like to apply, and determine their budgets accordingly from available funds, as well as the number of unemployed to be served and number of services. The second stage of selection occurs during work with the unemployed – the most appropriate instrument is matched to the needs of a particular person. This selection is made within the limits set in the annual plan (however, to some extent, there is some flexibility during the year).

Local offices also have instruments that enable them to adjust their actions to the needs of the local economy. They are allowed to spend up to 10% of their budget (Labour Fund) on special programmes, designed on the basis of an analysis of local needs. Special programmes consist of standard instruments and services, however up to 20% of the programme may be spent on specific forms of support, not envisaged in the Law. For example, the poviat labour office in Poznań recently has implemented two special programmes: Supporting Careers in Moving to Legal Employment and Supporting Terminated Employees.

These special programmes are a rather minor part of the activities of local offices. In fact, most offices concentrate on providing standard services for the general population of unemployed persons. Taking into account the fact that standard instruments are perceived to be sufficient in most cases, this approach seems to be rational.

Target groups and eligibility criteria. The Law on the Promotion of Employment specifies groups of unemployed in particularly difficult situation. However, about 90% of all unemployed persons fall into at least one of these groups, thus the task of prioritising and selecting targets groups is not carried out. In practice, poviat labour offices do not seem to plan based on target groups – in their annual plans, local offices focus on the types of instruments they plan to use, not on the types of unemployed persons who will be supported as a priority group. This approach is more flexible, but it may encourage "creaming" – selecting those persons for services who would more easily find a job.

With the new mechanism of profiling for unemployed persons (described in Chapter 2), the activities of poviat labour offices will focus on the unemployed who fall into the second profile. The persons in the first profile, who are considered to be closer to the labour market, would only receive a limited scope of support (job matching and in justified cases, job counselling, training, a grant or a loan for setting up a start-up, training or apprenticeship voucher). It is too early to assess the mechanism of profiling; however, during interviews and panel discussions, many respondents voiced a number of concerns, including:

- Profiling is based on an assessment conducted directly after the registration of a new person as unemployed, thus often the diagnosis is hasty and, in some cases, inadequate.
- The mechanism is based on tools developed by the Ministry of Family, Labour and Social Policy. And although the client advisors are able to modify the result of the profiling, it is not clear to what extent they in fact use this opportunity. In practice, evidence suggests that both unemployed persons and employment office staff are learning to cope with the new tool in order to achieve their objectives "in spite" of the system, instead of "in support" of it.
- Profiling may significantly reduce access to relevant labour market services, especially for those persons categorised to the third profile of support.

The last point was raised most often. The main instrument for this group is the Programme of Activation and Integration (PAI). Within this new mechanism, the most vulnerable unemployed persons should be supported by other institutions, primarily local social assistance centres, but also NGOs and employment agencies implementing PAI in co-operation with poviat labour offices. Unfortunately, social assistance centres lack the resources to provide support and to date, have been unwilling to implement new programmes. Additionally, representatives of the poviat labour offices noted that a significant part of the unemployed ascribed to the third profile of support are not in fact the clients of social assistance centres. Thus, thus even if local assistance centres implemented PAI, this would not cover those persons. Therefore, the majority of this group of unemployed was not covered by the new instrument.

For example, the programme was only implemented in each municipality (gmina) in just one of the eight poviats in the Radomski sub-region. However, this required much effort on the part of that poviat's labour office, and the programme was finally implemented by a local NGO. In other counties, the programme was implemented on a much more modest scale. For example, in the Radom municipality, only ten unemployed persons (out of over 30 000 registered unemployed persons) participated in this programme, while in Poznań, about 20 persons were involved. This is also confirmed by national data. About 461 000 unemployed were classified as third profile at the end of the August of 2015. During the first eight months of 2015, only 4 000 persons were covered by PAI, which is less than 1% of all classified as third profile (MLSP, 2015c). Despite this, poviat labour offices are not allowed to offer other forms of support to the unemployed in this profile category, even if they determine that it would be effective. As a result, the majority of persons in the most difficult situation were left without support.

Overall, the mechanism of profiling to target assistance seems to be going in the right direction in that it should support poviat labour offices in better targeting their actions (and limiting the risk of "creaming"). However, the mechanism would bring better results after implementing some improvements, especially in relation to the third profile.

In the case of the standard instruments of labour market policy, local office staff themselves decide to whom the instrument should be targeted, based on an assessment of needs and the potential of the unemployed, as well as the needs of the local labour market. For example, in the case of training programmes, there are three main methods of organising activities:

- The poviat labour office commissions training programmes for small groups of unemployed on the basis of assessing the needs of the local labour market and previous experience of the unemployed. Unemployed persons are directed to the training according to an assessment of their needs.
- Unemployed persons can apply to the poviat labour office for financing of the training, if they can prove that the training will help them find a job.
- A tripartite agreement is made between an employer, an unemployed person and the poviat labour office – the local office can finance the training of an unemployed person, adjusted to the needs of a particular employer, if the employer will hire him/her after the training.

According to the report of the poviat labour office in Poznań, 1 325 persons were trained, 76% in the form of group training, in 2014. Individual training was only provided for 155 persons. Also, according to the assessment of the poviat labour office in Radom, the majority of unemployed persons are directed to training in groups.

Budget management. The basic source of financing the Active Labour Market Policy in Poland is the Labour Fund, managed by the Ministry of Family, Labour and Social Policy. Another important source is the European Social Fund. However, from the perspective of poviat labour offices, there is no difference between these two sources. The Labour Fund is distributed to voivodeships on the basis of an algorithm. Governments at the voivodeship level then distribute the funds to the poviats based on the situation on the labour market.

Overall, poviat labour offices have the most flexibility in terms of budget compared to other aspects of management, with 30% of survey respondents reporting a high level of flexibility and 47% reporting some flexibility. Based on the voivodeship's distributions, the poviat labour office may independently plan how to spend its budget. Poviat labour offices prepare plans for the Labour Fund, indicating their spending for particular instruments. The financial plan is not linked to any performance indicators. The plan must be accepted by the Starosta (head of a poviat) and should also be discussed by the local labour council. However, in practice, poviat labour offices usually play the main role in this process. Any changes in the plan should go through the same procedure (opinion of the local labour market council and decision of the Starosta), so during the year, the flexibility of managing the Labour Fund is rather limited.

Performance management. In Poland, as was underlined during panel discussions with stakeholders, there is a long tradition of measuring the effectiveness of the active labour market policy. However, for a very long time, the measurement was seen as information to support management rather than as a performance indicator of local labour market policies. Recent reforms are bringing significant changes to this area. According to the Law on the promotion of employment, several key indicators were defined: 1) number of key staff in relation to number of unemployed; 2) effectiveness of key forms of supporting the unemployed (number of unemployed in employment) and 3) cost-effectiveness of key forms of supporting the unemployed (average unit cost of each form).

The Ministry of Family, Labour and Social Policy regularly monitors the performance of all poviat labour offices. Although the Ministry does not set specific targets for poviat offices, it compares their achievements, and those poviat labour offices achieving results above a certain threshold will receive bonuses for their staff. However, the threshold is based on the average for all poviat labour offices. Thus, this instrument provides a strong incentive for competition between poviat labour offices.

This arrangement was only introduced in 2014 and some temporary transition rules have been set. Thus, it is difficult to assess its impact. Some representatives of poviat labour offices emphasised the positive sides of this solution, such as increasing the motivation of employment offices while others expressed their scepticism. It was stated that the solution creates strong incentives for creaming, although this should be balanced (to some extent) by the mechanism of profiling.

The mechanism may also contribute to "creative accounting" in the poviat labour offices. The recent report of the Supreme Audit Office on activating the unemployed (SAO, 2015) provides evidence that the actual effectiveness of active labour market measures is significantly lower than that reported by the Ministry of Family, Labour and Social Policy. The main source of the difference is the methodology used to measure effectiveness adopted by the Ministry, which assumes that each person removed from the register upon completion of the measure is counted as effectively activated after a period of three months has passed since he/she left the programme. In practice, not all persons removed from the register are employed. Additionally, in some cases, employment may be unstable and the activated person may return to the employment offices. Thus, a more rigid methodology is required to also take into account the sustainability of employment (SAO, 2015).

The new mechanism also provides strong incentives to concentrate only on those activities directly contributing to the achievement of the indicators set in the Law. There is also a strong disincentive to invest resources in other, more innovative activities, such as, for example, improving the basic skills of the unemployed. Also, it does not allow for tailoring of performance metrics to local conditions, as evidenced by the fact that under 50% of poviat offices reported some or a high level of flexibility related to performance management.

By taking advantage of European Social Funds, poviat labour offices are obliged to comply with another set of performance management mechanisms. Poviat labour offices that implement projects financed by ESF are required to achieve a number of targets set by the Ministry of Economic Development (the Managing Authority for ESF in Poland). Performance indicators relate to the number of people in employment after project completion and are set for specific target groups. The indictors are at the same level for all poviat labour offices independently of the labour market situation. The indicators for the European Social Fund directly refer to the situation of clients upon leaving the projects (number of clients in employment upon leaving the project).

Contracting and outsourcing arrangements. Until recently, the scale of outsourcing services by public employment service offices was rather limited, due to a lack of interest by the public employment services to outsource their services and a lack of appropriate legal regulations. When surveyed, poviat labour offices reported that they had the least amount of flexibility in outsourcing and contracting compared to other aspects of management (but also indicated that additional flexibility in this aspect would be less useful than in other aspects of management).

As a result, the most common and standard practice is the outsourcing of training for unemployed persons. The training provider must be registered as a training institution. Training programmes are commissioned according to the Law on Public Procurement, mostly to private companies. Poviat labour offices determine the subject, duration, scope of training and number of persons trained. They also decide who will participate in the training. The poviat labour office determines most of the requirements of the training, and the contractor must present a detailed plan, which meets the requirements.

The recent reform of PES significantly changed the principles of outsourcing. The most important change is the introduction of a new mechanism: outsourcing at the regional level. This new approach was piloted in three voivodeships. In each of them, several poviats were involved. Conclusions from the pilot were ambiguous. The outcomes in terms of employment placement of the private service providers were below expectations, which may be explained by the relatively difficult group participating, the low quality of services and conditions of the tender (IBC, 2014). The new regulations took into account at least some of the conclusions from the pilot, and in the beginning of 2015, all regional employment offices launched tenders and commissioned the provision of services from private companies. The scale of outsourcing is not very large – usually the contracts are for services for 1 000-1 500 unemployed persons in each region. In the case of Wielkopolska, the number was 1 500. Each regional employment office prepares its own terms of reference. Although the Ministry of Family, Labour and Social Policy encouraged offices to provide contractors with as much flexibility as possible, the regional employment offices produced relatively detailed requirements for the contractors, including the types of unemployed to be targeted and types of services to be provided.

In the case of the Mazowiecki Region, services must include at minimum: the establishment of an activation centre in each poviat; a diagnosis of the situation of the unemployed; and the provision of at least two activation services. The contractor was obliged to present a detailed description of the proposed approach, and in addition to cost, the quality of the proposal was also assessed.

The most important part of the new approach is the mechanism of paying for results. Payment to the contractor depends on the results achieved and is made gradually:

- 20% after diagnosis,
- 20% for placement in employment for at least 14 days,
- 30% for placement in employment for at least 90 days,
- 30% for placement in employment for at least 180 days.

Thus, it is clear that Regional Employment offices are attempting to combine an approach of payment for results with attention to high quality services. It is too early to assess the outcome of this new approach. However, there is a need for further discussion, development and improvement of the mechanism. The most challenging aspects are the definition of results and the conditions of payment for services.

At the local level, poviat labour offices are allowed to outsource the social and vocational integration of unemployed persons classified to the third profile to NGOs in order to implement Programmes of Activation and Integration (PAI). Outsourcing is possible only if the local social assistance centre is not implementing PAI.

Flexibility in vocational education and training (VET)

As described in Chapter 1, all key elements of the education system are determined at the national level. However, management of the education system is delegated to local authorities. The Polish model of the management of education is perceived as the most decentralised in Europe (Herbst, 2012). As part of the delegation of daily management of schools to the local level, the lowest level of government (gmina) is responsible for primary and lower secondary schools, while the second level of government (poviat) is responsible for upper secondary education, including VET. Thus government at the county level is responsible for labour market policies and VET, which should provide for better co-ordination between these two areas. In practice, the level of co-ordination depends on the approaches of key local actors, as will be discussed later in the report.

Although many aspects of the education system are determined at the national level, there are still significant areas of flexibility at the poviat level to adjust VET to the needs of local labour markets. Local governments can influence the scope and quality of education in a number of areas, with the most important ones being:

- The structure of VET institutions operating locally (opening or closing schools as well as merging or dividing existing educational institutions);
- The selection of occupations taught at VET institutions amongst those defined by the classification of occupations for vocational education, developed by Ministry of National Education in co-operation with social partners (employers, sectoral organisations, etc.);
- Adaptation of the curriculum to the needs of local employers;
- Co-operation with local employers in terms of practical learning; and
- The quality of VET, including available equipment and number of teachers (to some extent).

In practice, these decisions are taken by school directors and by the local authorities supervising schools. However, the involvement of local authorities may differ, depending on the model of education management assumed at the local level. In some counties, school directors play a leading role, with the rather passive involvement of local authorities. In others, local authorities try to actively manage the offer of all educational institutions, adjusting it to the needs of the local labour market and coordinating it with the offer of vocational schools. The former model sometimes causes competition between VET institutions offering education and training in the same or similar occupations. This may also result in inadequate equipment in competing institutions: instead of one, well equipped workshop, providing practical training to all students in a particular occupation in the county, there are several underinvested workshops and, as a result, none of them is able to provide good quality education.

The Law on the Promotion of Employment and Labour Market Institutions regulates the formal mechanisms supporting the linkages between VET and the labour market: the Labour Market Council. These councils provide advice to local and regional employment offices. One of their tasks is issuing opinions on proposals for new professions to be taught in VET institutions.

Another issue is adjusting the curriculum to meet the specific needs of the local economy. For each qualification, the Ministry of National Education developed a core curriculum – a list of learning outcomes, divided into three categories: specific knowledge, skills and personal and social competence. VET institutions can autonomously design

Box 3.1. **Labour Market Councils – experience and the future**

In 2009, the Ministry of Labour and Social Policy conducted an assessment of the Labour Market Council for the period of 2004-2008. The research showed that councils fulfil the tasks set out in the Act, but in their advisory capacity, they have a rather limited impact on local labour market policy, and in many cases their work is rather formal and superficial. (MPiPS, 2009) The study does not explain the reasons behind this, but on the basis of the interviews and panel discussions, some may be indicated:

- a weak tradition of authentic social and civic dialogue and partnership at the local level,
- resistance of the employment offices' management to share their authority with other stakeholders,
- insufficient competences of members of the Labour Market Councils,
- insufficient quality and scope of information available to members of the councils needed to make any sound decisions on the policies of the labour market or vocational education.

In 2014, the amendment of the Act on Employment and Labour Market Institutions introduced some changes regarding the Labour Market Councils. The most important was the reduction in the number of council members, with a higher share of labour market representatives (employers). However, the basic assumption regarding the advisory role of labour councils was maintained. According to at least some representatives of the labour employment office, the new labour councils are increasingly more engaged and convinced about their ability to impact the labour market. For example, in one of the counties, the Labour Market Council negatively reviewed the new occupations proposed by VET institutions as being inadequate to the needs of the labour market. Unfortunately there is a lack of information whether those occupations were finally introduced or not.

Source: MLSP (2009), *Analiza działalności rad zatrudnienia i ich wpływ na kształtowanie polityki rynku pracy w okresie 2004-08; [The analysis of employment councils and their influence on policy the labour market in the period 2004-08]*, Ministry of Labour and Social Policy, Warsaw.

educational programmes on the basis of the core curriculum, which are adapted to the needs of the local labour market and employers. In practice, the scope of the adaptation varies among schools and depends on their approach and the history of their co-operation with employers. It should be noted here that developing their own programmes is still a challenge for many schools, thus a significant proportion of VET schools rely on the model programmes developed by the National Centre for Supporting Vocational and Continuing Education. These educational programmes are developed by professionals in close co-operation with practitioners and meet quality expectations, although they are not always adapted to the specific needs of local employers.

Capacities within the employment and VET sectors

Capacities in poviat labour offices

In Poland, there are two main sources of financing for the activities of poviat labour offices: the Labour Fund, managed by the Ministry of Family, Labour and Social Policy which mostly finances active labour market measures, and the resources of local government, which mostly finances labour market services provided by poviat labour offices (including staff costs). Expenditures for active labour market policies in Poland, measured as a percentage of GDP, is lower than the average in the EU28 and OECD countries but is higher than in many other central European countries (e.g. Lithuania, Latvia, Slovakia, the Czech Republic).

Figure 3.4. **Expenditures for the active labour market policy (percentage of GDP), Poland, 2005-13**

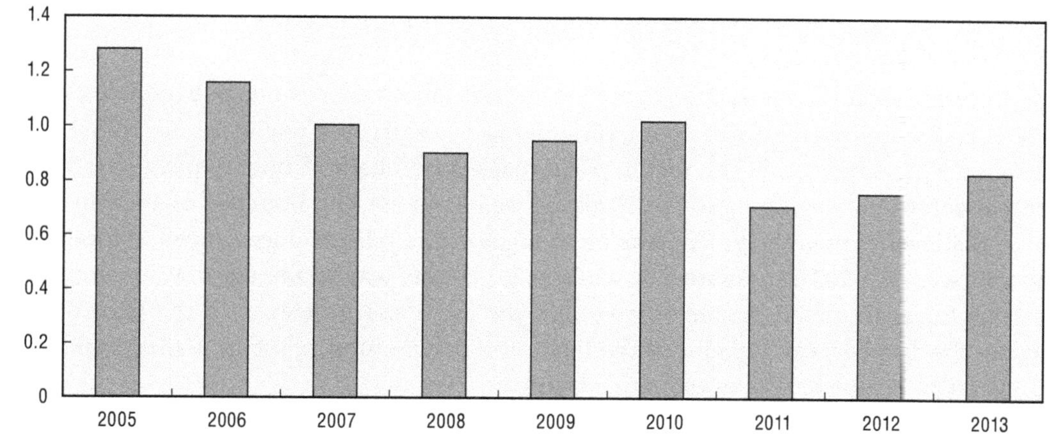

Source: Eurostat, Labour market policy database.

As presented in the graph above, expenditures for active labour market policies have in fact decreased during recent years. A significant reduction of spending is visible in 2011. This was the effect of a decision by the Ministry of Finance to freeze Labour Fund resources in order to improve the balance of public finances. However, this move significantly reduced the scope of active labour market policies. Since 2009, the first year of the financial crisis, there has been an increase in the number of registered unemployed and a decrease in the number of participants in active labour market policy activities (Figure 3.5). This clearly shows that spending on active labour market policies is pro-cyclical instead of anti-cyclical. As a result, the gap between the number of registered unemployed and the number of participants in active labour policy measures has been growing.

Figure 3.5. **Number of registered unemployed and number of participants in labour market policy measures, Poland, 2005-13**

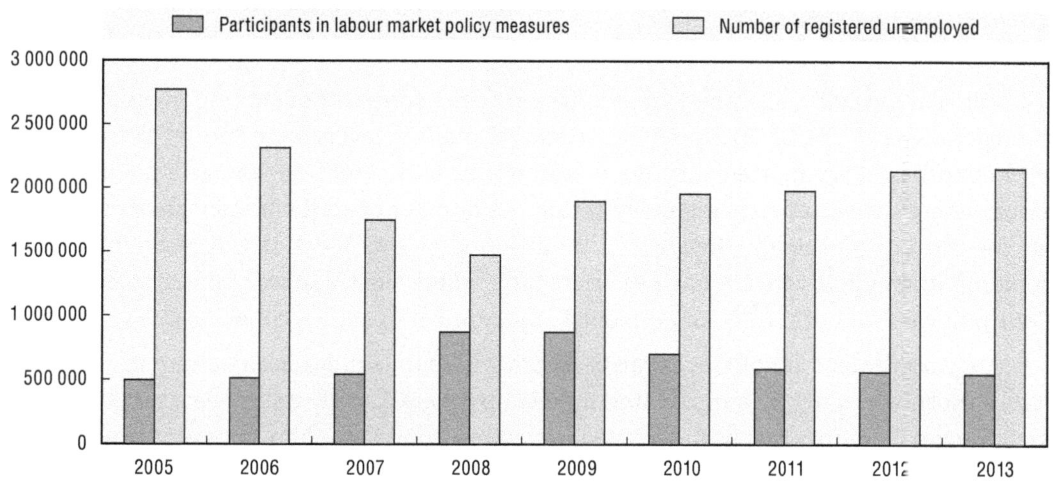

Source: Eurostat, Labour market policy database and Central Statistical Office, Local Data Bank.

Despite the problems described above, poviat labour office representatives declare that the resources available for active labour market policy measures (from the Labour Fund) are sufficient. Due to administrative burdens, it would be difficult to manage significantly greater resources with the current number of employees in local offices. On the other hand, resources for services from local budgets are assessed as insufficient. Underinvestment limits the number of employees of poviat labour offices and reduces their capacity.

In terms of staff levels, the capacity of poviat labour offices has been stable during recent years and oscillates at about 100 unemployed per one poviat labour office staff member. This situation is the result of decreasing numbers of unemployed persons in comparison to the beginning of the 2000s, as well as increasing numbers of staff. In 2002, when the level of unemployment was at its highest, the ratio of unemployed to local staff capacity was over 200 (see Figure 3.6), while in 2014, there was an average of 95 unemployed persons for each poviat labour office employee in Poland. However, in the Mazowiecki Region, the number was 121 (one of the highest in the country), while in Wielkopolska, the number was 78, one of the lowest in the country.

Figure 3.6. **Number of registered unemployed persons per each employee in the poviat labour office, Poland, 2000-14**

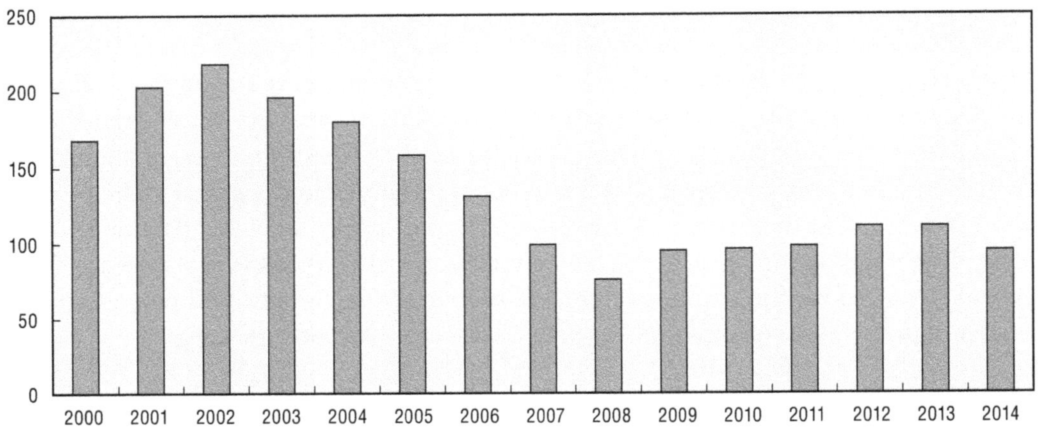

Source: MLSP, 2015b, *Information on staffing and the structure of employment in regional and poviat labour offices in 2014*, Ministry of Labour and Social Policy.

The opinions of local employment offices as to the adequacy of staffing levels differ. 25% of respondents to the OECD Survey reported that staffing levels were "not at all sufficient" while another 33% reported they were "somewhat sufficient". In Poznań's poviat labour office, where the situation is relatively better, the number of staff was considered sufficient for the current workload. However, if maintained at this level, it would be difficult to implement new, innovative measures. In Radom, where the situation is much worse (about 100 employees for over 30 000 unemployed), the number of staff is considered insufficient.

Another dimension of the capacity of poviat labour offices is the share of front-line staff – those who directly support unemployed persons. During recent years, the share of this category of employees has increased, reflecting improvement in access to professional labour market services, such as counselling.

Looking at staff capacities, PES staff members have traditionally been intensively trained. In 2014, 80% of employment office employees took part in training or education. In the opinion of representatives of employment offices, their staff's competences are considered adequate at the very least.

These findings are also reflected in the survey of employment offices undertaken as part of this project. According to a self-assessment, the level of knowledge on the labour market and skills of employees are mostly adequate and sufficient. However, the insufficient number of staff (at least in some poviat labour offices) and scarce resources to implement active labour market policy measures make it difficult to adjust to the needs of the local economy (see Figure 3.7).

Figure 3.7. **The assessment of available resources for the poviat labour office, 2015**

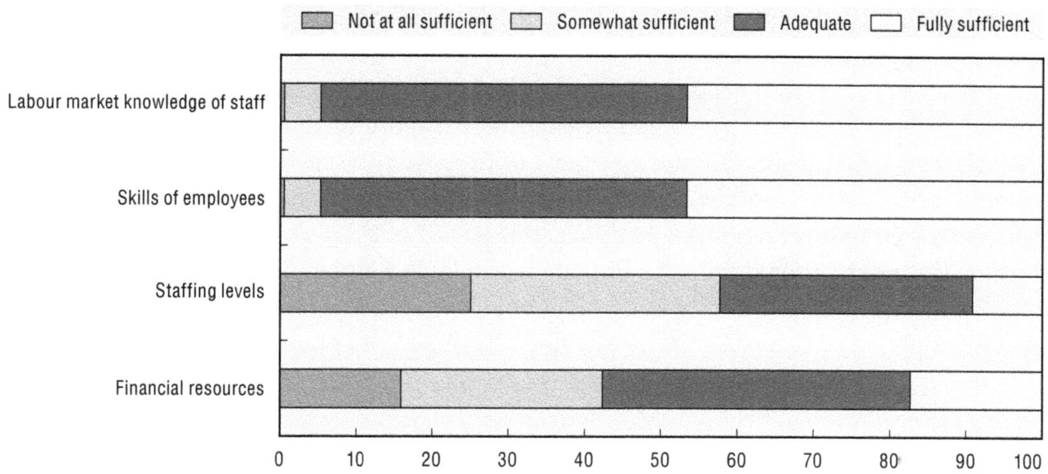

Source: OECD LEED survey of poviat labour offices.

Capacities within vocational education and training

Providing high quality vocational education and training requires a significant investment of resources, and adapting to the changing needs of the local economy and labour market requires additional resources. The insufficient capacity of VET institutions can hinder this adaptation, causing VET to permanently lag behind labour market changes.

Public expenditures for IVET as a percentage of GDP (0.57%) is lower than the EU average of 0.68% (2011 data). The amount spent per student (EUR 4 330) is also below the EU average of 8 586 EUR (CEDEFOP, 2015). VET education is financed by local government at the poviat level, from state budget subventions. The subvention for the county is calculated on the basis of the number of students continuing their education.

Although education is one of the major areas of spending by local authorities, VET institutions are seen as being significantly underinvested in. Most of the respondents and panel participants pointed out that the equipment in workshops for practical learning is often out of date and the materials necessary for training and practical education are insufficient. According to the assessment of the National Centre of Supporting Vocational and Continuous Education, around one-fourth of schools do not have any workshops for practical education and training (NCSVCE, 2013). The Teaching and Learning International Survey TALIS 2013 showed that teachers viewed instructional materials (two-third of teachers in VET) and computers for instruction (50% in basic vocational schools and 37% in technical upper secondary schools) as the most important deficiencies in education. The numbers in these categories are significantly higher than for other types of schools in Poland and the averages for other countries participating in the study (IER, 2014). Lack of instructional materials hampers the quality of teaching and the ability to adjust to the needs of the labour market.

On the other hand, the vast majority of schools have been modernising their workshops and rooms for practical training over the past five years, with over half of this work occurring in the previous two years. Additionally, according to a monitoring of the implementation of the new core curriculum for vocational education, the majority of schools had investments planned in the forthcoming year (NCSVET, 2015). This shows that most local authorities are aware of the need for investments in vocational education (most of the counties investing in VET used their own funds), and though still unsatisfactory, the situation has been improving.

Additionally, during the panel discussions, participants underscored that some counties, especially smaller ones, and those outside of major cities, lack sufficient capacity and resources to invest in good infrastructure and offer good quality VET. The co-operation of local and regional authorities can be especially important in such cases, as it is more efficient to plan and implement a system of high quality vocational education at the regional level. In a few regions, authorities have undertaken such an effort. A decision was made to invest in a number of vocational centres (schools for youth and adult education centres), in order to maximise the impact of available European funds and significantly improve the conditions and quality of vocational learning. The textbox below provides one such example, in addition to other strategies being used to improve VET.

Box 3.2. **Examples of approaches to improving VET capacities**

Strengthening individual schools. One example is a vocational institution in Swarzędz, close to Poznań, that provides vocational education for youth and adults. The institution is generously supported by the local government, very well equipped and offers, according to local actors, very good quality vocational education. The school also has strategic partners, Volkswagen and Solaris, two large companies that significantly impact not only the educational programmes, but also the process of learning. Yet, it should also be mentioned that the process of initiating co-operation between employers and the VET school was a long one and at the very beginning, there was much resistance on the part of the schools.

Setting up vocational laboratories. Regional and local authorities are also looking for innovative solutions to improve the capacity of VET institutions. One example is the creation of several laboratories for vocational education (financed by the European Social Fund). The laboratories were designed as very innovative and modern facilities intended for practical vocational education. It was assumed that the equipment in the laboratories should be better than what is found on the market in order to prepare students for future labour market needs. The laboratories can be used by VET students from schools across the entire region. The standard training in such a laboratory takes one week for a group of students. VET teachers also take part in this training. The laboratories are set occupations such as information technology technician, merchant, logistics, economist, mechatronics, techniques and organisation of advertisement.

Taking a regional approach. In the Dolnośląski Region, the regional authorities have diagnosed a number of deficiencies in vocational education. On this basis, they planned a regional programme of vocational education development, including the selection of seven economic sectors of special importance for the regional labour market, and then set up vocational training centres related to these sectors in nine counties. The distribution of the centres was spread evenly throughout the region. The Programme included investments in infrastructure (modern equipment for vocational education), as well as investments in the

Box 3.2. **Examples of approaches to improving VET capacities** *(cont.)*

competences of teachers and students (additional lessons for students, intensive co-operation with local employers, educational and vocational counselling for students).

This programme is a good example of the co-ordination of VET development in a region, which requires the establishment of a good partnership among regional and local authorities, implementation in a planned and systematic manner, and a selective approach to the improvement of the quality of vocational education. It is also an example of good co-ordination between different instruments: investments in the infrastructure were financed by the European Regional Development Fund (ERDF), while investments in competences were finance by the European Social Fund (ESF).

Beyond equipment, the main challenge for VET is the capacity of teachers. According to many studies, the qualifications of VET teachers is one of the main factors that influences the quality of teaching, as well as the profile of VET education (Hattie, 2009). In many cases, their skills determine the scope to adjust VET to labour market needs. This can be analysed at the level of the whole school (the extent to which occupation profiles match the needs of the labour market), as well as at the level of particular teachers (the extent to which their classes and the skills taught address labour market needs). In fact, there is a rather limited scope of research on teachers in VET (there is much higher interest in the skills of teacher in general education).

In Poland, the population of teachers is becoming older and in 2010, almost 70% of VET institutions reported problems with recruiting new teachers, mostly due to the lack of appropriate candidates. Working conditions, especially wages in VET, are at a relatively low level in comparison to the industrial sector, which makes it very difficult to attract professionals with practical experience. This problem may be more significant in large cities such as Poznań, where the wages offered in the private sector are much more attractive (NCSVET, 2013). Additionally, a significant number of VET teachers themselves do not have sufficient practical experience nor the skills needed on the labour market. A significant proportion of them have very limited contact with actual work places and limited knowledge about currently used technologies and equipment. This is mostly due to the rather limited connections between schools and the labour market. As a solution, some VET institutions invite practitioners from industry to work with them.

Policy co-ordination, policy integration and co-operation with other sectors

Policy co-ordination, integration and communication between different actors is a key contributor to being able to adapt and implement policies in response to the changing needs of the labour market and economic development. However, the extent to which this is happening in the local case study areas seems to vary. There are some examples of good co-operation, but these are often formal and superficial, based on the motivation of individual persons or limited to the basic exchange of information.

Linkages between labour market policy, vocational education and economic development

At the very heart of this study is the co-operation between actors in the areas of the labour market, vocational education, and economic development. As the study shows, the co-ordination of these policies heavily depends on the attitudes and initiatives of individual persons and institutions, but these "individual" factors should be supported by institutionalised mechanisms. As previously described, one such mechanism is the labour market council, which consists of representatives of employers' organisations, trade unions, farmers' organisations and non-governmental organisations. Local authorities can also invite representatives of local government and researchers to the council. In some labour market councils, representatives of the local administration responsible for VET and economic development also participate, however this is not the rule.

Linkages between local labour market policy, vocational education and economic development policy are often driven by interactions between the persons responsible for these areas within the local administration. This is more typically the case for economic development and education – their contacts occur more often and are more intensive (e.g. they consult ideas of new projects, prepare joint programmes and projects). The co-operation is also intensive in situations such as new investments. This type of co-operation, more ad-hoc and based on personal relations, is more typical for Radom than Poznań.

Examples of new mechanisms developed in order to enhance more systematic co-operation between these sectors also exist. One example is a new initiative in Radom – the Cluster of Vocational Education.

Box 3.3. **Clusters of Vocational Education as an example of mechanism supporting co-operation of VET with labour market**

The idea of clusters of vocational education is relatively new and was initiated by the recent amendments of the Law on the Special Economic Areas, which made the companies managing special economic areas responsible for establishing such clusters. The main idea is to create a mechanism for regular co-operation between vocational education, employers and other actors (including labour market institutions). According to information on the web page of the Ministry of Economic Development, there are about 11 such clusters in Poland, with this number likely to increase.

The cluster in Radom was established in June 2015 and project development was still in the early stages at the time of this research. Some activities have already been undertaken to build the relationships between VET institutions and enterprises operating in the Special Economic Area, including analysing the educational offer of VET institutions against needs of local employers. It is assumed that in the future the cluster will act as facilitator to support the modernisation of vocational education in line with the needs of local enterprises and facilitate the access of students and teachers to modern infrastructure, etc.

Source: Tarnobrzeg Special Economic Area, *www.tsse.arp.pl/aktualnosci/radom-stawia-na-zawodowcow-kolejny-klaster-edukacji-zawodowej-przy-tsse-euro-park-wislosan.*

During the study visit, a number of other forms of co-operation were identified, including:

- The Programme Board of the Observatory of Economy and Education of the Poznań Agglomeration, where representatives of policy makers responsible for education participate, as well as employers, representatives of higher education institutions, and trade unions.
- The network supporting entrepreneurship and employment, established in 2002 in Poznań. All key actors participate (local government authorities responsible for economic development, employers' organisations, academic organisations, units supporting entrepreneurship, poviat and regional labour offices, and the social insurance office).

- Poznań's Centre for Entrepreneurship Support, established by local authorities in 1993 within the structure of the poviat labour office, is responsible for supporting start-ups and existing micro and small enterprises.

Box 3.4. **Poznań Centre for Entrepreneurship Support**

The centre was established in 1993 by the local authorities and since then has operated as a part of the poviat labour office. Its main objective has been to support entrepreneurship through boosting the number of small and medium enterprises and improving their competitiveness.

The Centre provides counselling and training services to start-ups and existing small enterprises. For example, it offers information on how to start a business such as choosing the form of activity, determining the profile of the future of the company, getting to know the sources of financing, learning how to prepare a business plan and gathering the necessary documentation when applying for a grant or a loan to start the company. The Centre offers also consultations with a tax advisor, accountant, lawyer, and specialist in marketing and sales. These services are provided by the staff of the Centre as well as experts from local institutions (tax office, labour inspections, social insurance institutions). The trainings offered by the Centre focus on similar topics (tax and social insurance regulations, accounting, marketing).

Another interesting practise is the Micro-entrepreneurs Club, targeted to people who received a grant from the poviat labour office to establish a new business. Apart from traditional counselling and trainings, the Club facilitates networking and exchange of experience among new entrepreneurs.

Source: Poznań Centre for Entrepreneurship Support, *www.powp.poznan.pl*.

It is worth stressing that these types of practices seem to be more typical in the Poznań sub-region. This may be related to a tradition of co-operation still present in Wielkopolska region, where Poznań is located, and less prevalent in the Mazowiecki Region, where Radom is located.

Strategic documents also provide an indication of how these policies are coordinated. Another model is the development of one general strategy for a territory. In Poznań, there is one main strategy of development for the city to 2030, recently updated in 2013. The strategy focusses on economic development, attracting investors, the quality of academic institutions, and the quality of life. However, there are no references to labour market policies or VET. There is one objective related to education, but this relates to the quality of life priority and mostly refers to the quality of general education without mentioning vocational education.

Strategies are also prepared at the poviat level. An example is the "Strategy for sustainable development of Radomski County". The strategy covers economic development, the labour market, education and a number of other areas. However, the strategy is rather general and describes proposed actions, which would have been done anyway by local actors. The strategy also contains a multi-annual investment plan. The plan focusses mostly on infrastructure investments. Investments in the education sector are limited to a sports facility in one upper secondary school. These examples clearly show that although different forms of co-operation take place, a strategic, long-term perspective of integrating these sectors is lacking.

Co-ordination between poviat labour offices and other labour market actors

In the case of local labour market policies, the central actor is the poviat labour office. While these offices are part of the local administration as discussed earlier, in many cases the poviat labour office is perceived as a separate office instead of as part of local government, and thus is not seen as being co-responsible for local development policy.

As explained in chapter two, local labour market policies are implemented by other actors as well. Although poviat labour offices play a key role in providing services for job-seekers and employers, they should also actively coordinate the efforts of all other actors involved in this field. Again, the picture emerging from this research is ambiguous. Although the vast majority of poviat labour offices declare that they co-operate with other actors in some way, this co-operation seems superficial in many cases. In practice, poviat labour offices seem to be focused on their own activities, communicating with other institutions, and tend to pay rather limited attention to the actions of different actors working in the same or similar areas. According to respondents, poviat labour offices are willing to co-operate but do not initiate such activities nor do they try to coordinate the actions of different actors.

Where co-ordination does occur, it is often another institution (e.g. a local NGO) working on labour market issues that initiates the relationship with the poviat labour office, with the poviat labour office playing a more passive role. For example, several NGOs in Poznań approached the poviat labour office concerning a project to help disadvantaged jobseekers set up a new social enterprise. The NGOs worked with the participants to help them set-up the social enterprise, and the poviat labour office provided a grant to establish this social enterprise.

Of particular interest is the co-operation with employers. On one hand, the majority of employment offices declared that they co-operate intensively with this group. On the other hand, most of them declared in a 2008 study that employers and their organisations have limited impact on employment office objectives and activities (MLSP, 2008). This can be explained by the nature of the co-operation with employers – in most cases, it relates to the needs of particular employers or unemployed persons (e.g. matching employers with the unemployed, improving the competences of unemployed persons according to the needs of an employer).

A higher level of co-operation would imply increased employer involvement in shaping labour market policies. Employers are represented in local labour councils, which play an advisory role in most cases. Members of the councils may express their opinion, and suggest some changes in the structure of the budget. However, in practice, there is strong resistance among poviat labour office representatives to transfer even part of their authority to the councils.

In Poland, co-operation between labour offices and social assistance centres is strongly emphasised. These institutions often have an overlapping client group, as people very often use labour market and social assistance services simultaneously. There is a growing understanding that the efforts of both institutions should be highly coordinated to avoid segmented and ineffective services. The effort to improve the level of co-ordination is taken at the national as well as the local level. At the national level, co-operation is encouraged by several regulations in the legal acts governing these two areas. At the local level, many institutions have established some form of co-operation, from the very basic (exchange of information) to the more complex (joint projects and programmes). In the

2015 OECD LEED survey, 58% of public employment service respondents reported that they have comprehensive joint programme or strategy development with welfare and social integration institutions, a category which includes social assistance centres.

These observations are also confirmed by the quantitative results of the survey of poviat labour offices. About 60% of poviat labour offices declared that they do not work with or only share information with private sector employment agencies and non-governmental organisations. Only 20% of them declared that they are operating joint programmes or strategies with such partners. Co-operation occurs more often and is more substantial in the case of training facilities (27% report co-ordination or joint programme or strategy development). The most prevalent and substantial type of co-operation is working with employers: 60% of poviat labour offices declared that they had developed joint programmes or strategies with this group. Poviat labour offices were least likely to work with schools and universities (post-secondary schools, state higher schools of vocational education, universities, and vocational schools) and regional or local economic development agencies.

Figure 3.8. **Intensity of local collaboration of poviat labour offices, Poland, 2015**

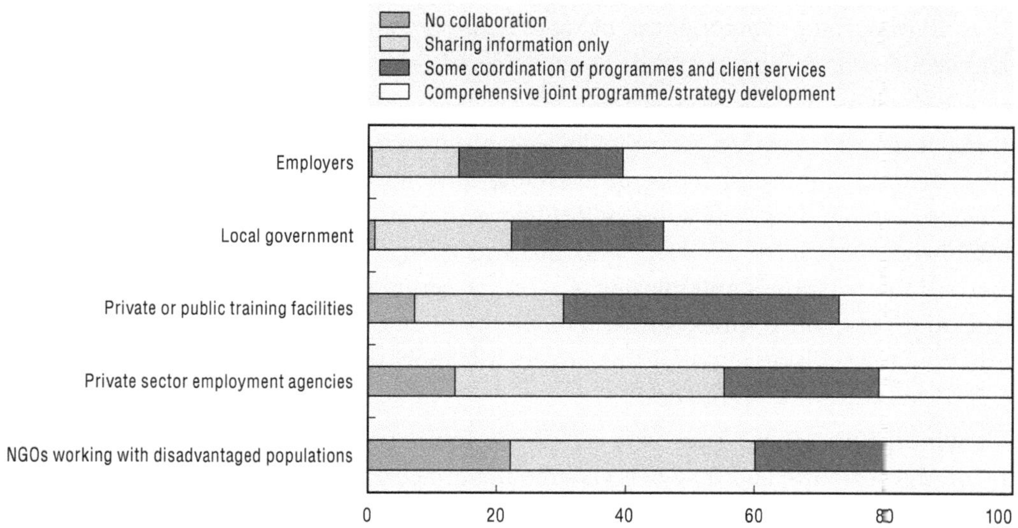

Source: 2015 OECD LEED survey to poviat labour offices.

This contrasts somewhat with the findings from a 2008 study, in which poviat labour offices were asked about the impact of different types of institutions on their activities. For each type of institution, the graph below presents the percentage of local offices that reported that institution had a rather large or large impact on the office's objectives and activities. Poviat labour offices reported that local authorities had the most significant impact, while other actors of the labour market (employers, NGOs, local labour councils) had a more limited impact.

Evidence based policy making

Use of up-to-date, locally specific data

One of the main justifications for local flexibility and decentralisation is that local actors have better knowledge about the local situation, and so are able to better manage local policies and adjust them to local needs. However, the availability of good quality local

Figure 3.9. **The percentage of poviat labour offices which declare that particular type of institution have rather large or large impact on their objective and activity, Poland, 2008**

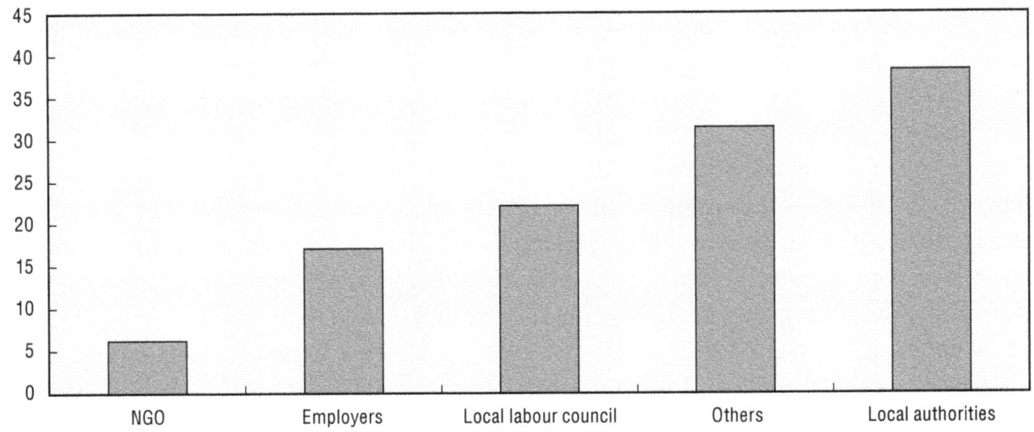

Source: MLSP (2008), *Analiza funkcjonowania urzędów pracy po ich włączeniu do administracji samorządowej*, Ministry of Labour and Social Policy, Warsaw.

data is an important component of being able to plan and implement policy strategically. In this section, several types of data are considered.

In Poland, the scope of statistical data collected through surveys is decided at the national level, and there is a variety of local level data available in almost all areas of public policy. Despite the broad scope of available data about the local level, a number of challenges remain: in practice, many local governments are not aware of the data that is available; the capacity for data analysis and interpretation is not sufficient; some important information is still missing (e.g. on the actual number and characteristics of job offers); and the quality, timeliness and reliability of data is not sufficient. For example, in conducting the skills analysis for this project, the most recently available data available at the TL3 level was for the year 2011.

Poviat labour offices have very detailed administrative data (as opposed to survey data) on the structure and flow of registered unemployed persons as well as registered job vacancies. The most important areas of data include:

- Information on the structure of registered unemployed persons (age, education, previous professional experience, disability, residence, etc.) – changes and status;
- Information on the number of unemployed persons engaged in active labour market policy measures;
- Information on the costs of active labour market policy measures;
- Information on the effectiveness of active labour market policy measures (number of persons in employment three months after leaving active labour market policy measures); and
- Information on the number and characteristics of job vacancies registered in the local labour market.

This type of administrative data is regularly analysed. For example, poviat labour offices produce a detailed annual report about the situation on the local labour market, focused on unemployment and local labour market policies. The report does not analyse other aspects of the labour market, such as employment, skills, vocational education, adult education, and migration. This illustrates an issue raised by other researchers: poviat labour offices tend to only focus on registered unemployment and are less interested in other aspects of the labour market.

There is also a rather detailed scope of information available for both local authorities and VET institutions on the VET sector. The scope of this data covers such areas as:

- The capacity of VET institutions (number of teachers, rooms, and financial situation);
- Number of students in each VET institution and in particular occupations (especially new students, as well as the proportion of VET students among all students, which is evidence of the attractiveness of VET); and
- Number of graduates passing vocational exams for each occupation taught, as well as the results of general exams (this concerns only technical upper secondary school students).

Although representatives of both types of institutions declared that they intensively use available data, it is acknowledged that more substantial information should be provided. Both local and regional authorities have undertaken several initiatives in order to provide more informative data. One such example is described in more detail in the textbox below.

Box 3.5. **Monitoring situation of the graduates of all upper secondary and higher education institutions in Poznań**

The poviat labour office in Poznań regularly prepares a report on the situation of the graduates of all upper secondary and higher education institutions in Poznań. The report provides detailed information on the number of graduates registered as unemployed and its relationship to the total number of graduates as well as on the number (and percentage) of students, having taken a job six months from graduating and one year from graduating. The data are presented for particular occupations and for each school in Poznań. The report has been produced every year since 2001 and, it is reported that representatives of VET institutions are very interested in its results. This report is a positive example of combining data for VET and the poviat labour office to produce informative analyses to support the decisions of youth and their parents. On the other hand, as far as the research team was able to determine from the collected information, this initiative is unique in the country. It should also be noted that the report only provides information on a small proportion of students – those who are registered as unemployed. It does not provide any information about the situation of other students, such as their occupations and wages, which would be much more informative for local policy makers, as well as parents and students.

Source: www.absolwenci.poznan.pl.

Although many interviewers agreed that this sort of information is crucial for adequate labour market, there is not enough information on the supply and demand for skills, both in the present and in the future available at the local level. However, there are some examples of efforts undertaken in this area. The most important one is the regular monitoring of surplus and deficit occupations, which is conducted by each poviat labour office every six months. The Ministry of Family, Labour and Social Policy developed a monitoring methodology that allows the results to be aggregated at the regional and national levels. The main objective of the monitoring is to compare the recent occupations of registered unemployed persons and the job offers listed in poviat labour offices. The monitoring has a number of strengths, including:

- Detail: the monitoring is based on the Classification of Occupations and Specialisations for the labour market, developed by the Ministry of Family, Labour and Social Policy, and the results are available at the lowest level of classification – occupations (six digit codes);
- Regularity: it is regularly conducted every six months, thus data are comparable over time; and
- Aggregation: the data can be aggregated from the local level to the national level.

But the monitoring also has some weaknesses:

- It is only based on the job offers registered in the poviat labour office – it is estimated that only about 20-30% of all job offers are registered in poviat labour offices;
- The job offers submitted to the labour offices are segmented – employers more often submit job offers for manual workers and low-skilled service jobs (Kocór et al., 2015); and
- It is based on the last job held by unemployed persons, which may be misleading and provide inaccurate information, as it does not provide information on the actual skills and qualifications of unemployed persons. A person lacking a formal diploma or certificate is categorised as not having qualifications.

Because of the above-mentioned issues, respondents during interviews and study visits note that the instrument is only partially useful. Thus, numerous other initiatives that provide more accurate information on the supply and demand of labour market skills are undertaken at the national and regional levels.

As mentioned earlier, the Observatory of the Economy and Labour Market of the Poznań Agglomeration, which collects information on the labour market, economy and education, conducts its own research, such as *The need for employers of the businesses of the Poznań agglomeration,* and *Two worlds: vocational education and the needs of the local economy*.

Another example is the Regional Observatory of the Labour Market for the Wielkopolska Region, which conducts a study on the *Needs of the Regional Labour Market for Qualifications and Competences* (ROLMW, 2014), that presents analyses for sectors and sub-regions. Also, the Regional Observatory of the Labour Market in the Mazowiecki Region conducts surveys on skills gaps. Recent research, conducted in 2013, analysed branches and sub-regions for skills gaps. However, due to the very broad scope of the research, the results were rather general and had limited use for local stakeholders. It should be also noted that the research conducted focused strongly on the demand side and provided little evidence of the supply side (the actual competences of graduates, employees and unemployed persons) (MLMO, 2015).

From the discussion, it is clear that the system of monitoring and forecasting skills supply and demand should be further improved and developed in order to provide more in-depth and accurate information at the regional as well as the local level. The studies also need to be more specific, such as by concentrating on specific sectors or occupations. Some support in this regard may be provided by sectoral skills councils, which will be established at the national level by the Polish Agency of Enterprise Development in close co-operation with social partners. The risk is that the councils will concentrate on the national level and leave regional and sub-regional labour markets with an insufficient scope of information.

Managing skills supply and demand at the local level also requires good knowledge about skills within both administrative boundaries and local travel to work areas. In practice, local authorities are usually aware of migration and travel to work patterns; however, they have limited access to more detailed data on the scale and structure of the travel to work and its impact on the labour market. Analysing the local travel to work area is rather complicated because standardised information on the labour market is usually only available at the level of neighbouring administrative units, which do not always correspond to the "travel to work" area. It is also possible to retrieve more detailed statistics of travel to work areas from administrative sources (e.g. the tax office, employment office), but, this requires more effort and co-operation. Available data tends to focus on the situation in particular administrative units and do not provide information on the skills and competences of the persons flowing between them.

Evaluation evidence

Evaluations are conducted mostly at the regional or national level and are generally performed on the activities financed by European funds, namely: active labour market policy measures (e.g. activities addressed to the elderly or youth); education; social integration; and also economic development. The number of evaluations has rapidly increased during recent years, mostly because they are required and European funds are available to finance them. However, knowledge about and utilisation of these evaluations at the local level seems to be rather limited, mostly due to the limited involvement of local partners in the evaluation process. In many cases, the conclusions and recommendations of evaluations are not used in the policy making process.

Poviat labour offices regularly monitor the effectiveness of active labour market policy measures and some of them regularly publish the results. However, the effectiveness of their support is measured only three months after the end of participation in the services. This short period is not sufficient for a reliable assessment of the effectiveness of labour market programmes. Additionally, local institutions very rarely conduct a professional, rigorous evaluation of their activities. In fact, in the course of this study, only one example of an evaluation conducted by the poviat labour office in Radom was identified (which was not publicly available). The report focused on the sustainability of new enterprises, established by grants, and new subsidised job positions. The research showed that sustainability after four years was very high (85%); however in some cases, sustainability was significantly lower. Conclusions from the research were used to improve the practices of the poviat labour office.

Theme 2: Adding value through skills

Figure 3.10. **Dashboard results: Adding value through skills**

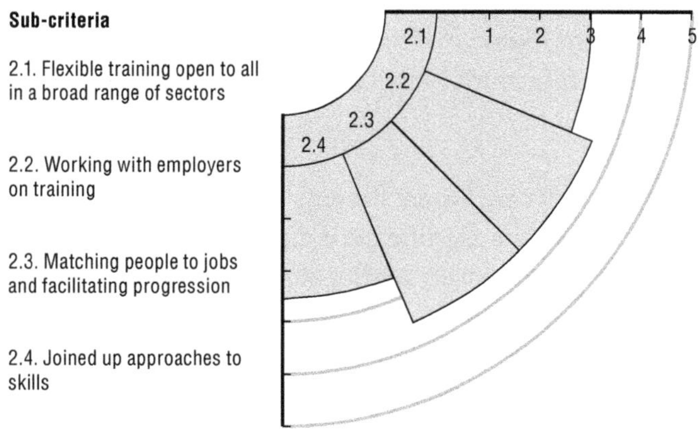

Flexible training open to all in a broad range of sectors

Participation in lifelong learning

In Poland, participation of adults in lifelong learning is particularly low – PIAAC research indicates that 35% of adults aged 25-64 in Poland participated in formal or non-formal education in 2012, compared to an average of 51% across surveyed countries (OECD, 2014). National data from Poland that measures participation in education and training shows that participation rates have remained the same for many years, despite public investment in this area. In fact, the data for recent years shows a noticeable decline in lifelong learning participation between 2010 and 2011. This may be linked with a decline in the number of unemployed persons participating in training and education, caused by cuts in the Labour Fund; however, this issue requires further examination.

Figure 3.11. **Participation in education and training in the four weeks prior to the survey for person aged 25-64, Mazowiecki and Wielkopolska Regions in comparison to Poland, 2001-2014**

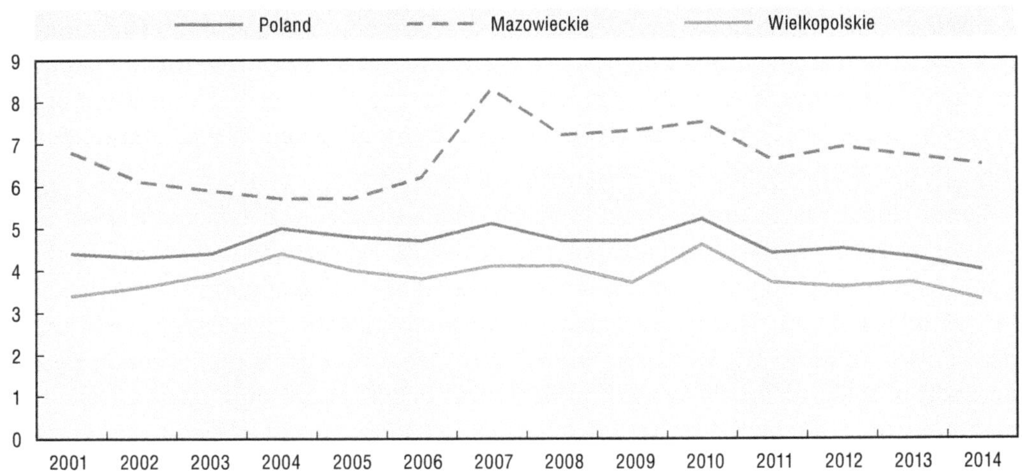

Source: Central Statistical Office, Labour Force Survey.

In regard to the case study areas, data is only available at the regional level. As presented in the graph above, the participation rate is higher in the Mazowiecki Region compared to the situation in the Wielkopolska Region. Moreover, in recent years, the gap between these two regions has widened. However, in case of the Mazowiecki Region, the high value is almost certainly generated by Warsaw itself, and actual data for the Radomski sub-region are significantly lower. On the other hand, in the case of Wielkopolska, the situation in Poznań is probably much better than in other parts of that region.

Availability of courses

While there are a range of non-formal training courses available in both Poznań and the Radomski sub-regions, there are significant differences between these two areas. The education market in Poznań is very well developed, while in Radom, the offer is much more modest. An example of this is the information provided on the portal *www.inwestycjewkadry.pl* [*Investment in Staff*], which provides information on available training opportunities. In September 2015, there were 875 training opportunities for Poznań, and only 51 for Radom.

Although the numbers should be interpreted as a proxy for the scale of the training market (the portal contains only a certain portion of all training opportunities), this clearly shows the differences between these two cities.

Also, studies conducted by the Regional Observatory of the Labour Market for the Mazowiecki Region confirm that the scope of courses offered in the Radomski sub-region are rather limited, especially outside of Radom. A comprehensive assessment of the offer is rather difficult, due to the fact that there is a lack of current, widely available information on training courses and the scope of VET education for adults at the regional and sub-regional levels. This also makes it difficult for both employers and training candidates to find the resources to meet their needs.[1]

Institutions offering courses and training are usually concentrated in larger cities, thus access for persons living outside of urban areas may be more difficult. This is the case for the Radomski sub-region, where two-thirds of all courses in 2011 were available in Radom (MLMO, 2011a) and persons from other districts have to travel to take part in courses. This also applies to vocational education. In other districts of the Radomski sub-region, the range of VET is much more limited. According to the research conducted by the Mozowiecki Observatory of the Labour Market, 56% of students from Lipski County in the last class of lower secondary education (before choosing VET) plan to select a school in another city and among them, almost half plan to move to another city. Most of them indicated Zwoleń (a neighbouring city) or Radom (MLMO, 2011a). In the Wielkopolska region, there were about 1 200 registered training institutions (mostly private), with one third of them registered in Poznań. This clearly shows the high concentration of training offers in the capital of this region.

Vocational, formal education for adults has historically been provided by vocational schools for adults (basic and upper secondary). However, during recent years, the number of students in these schools has significantly decreased, mostly due to the introduction of a new, more flexible form of vocational education for adults known as vocational qualifications courses. This new form was introduced in 2012 and is part of the vocational education reform described in the second chapter of this report. In the 2013/2014 school year, 16 000 adults participated in educational programmes organised by vocational secondary schools for adults, other educational institutions (e.g. centres of practical education or centres of continuing education), as well as post-secondary schools and colleges.

Another instrument of making training more flexible to meet the needs of learners is the modular approach, where training is divided into separate, independent modules, adjusted to particular skills or vocational tasks. What is particularly important is the merging of theoretical and practical learning in one unit. The teacher provides the necessary theoretical information, which is consequently tested in practice by students. Previously the insufficient correlation of theoretical and practical learning was in many cases indicated as one of the weaknesses of traditional vocational education.

Despite its strengths, the implementation of modular education in VET has met a number of barriers related to the organisation of education, competences of teachers, and equipment in schools. In order to minimise these barriers, a number of measures have been undertaken at the national and local level in order to support this approach. Modular education is also strongly supported by the National Centre for Supporting Vocational and Continuing Education, which provides guidelines, examples of curriculum, training for directors and teachers. In Wielkopolska, 35 vocational schools have implemented this new

Box 3.6. Vocational qualifications courses in the Centre for Practical Education in Radom

It was assumed that the centres for practical education would serve as a common site for practical learning for different schools from a certain area (usually a county). In practice, vocational schools used these facilities only partially, preferring to invest in their own workshops (which in many cases was caused by the insufficient co-ordination of vocational education at the local level). The situation was the same for the Centre for Practical Education in Radom, whose capacity was only partially used.

In 2012, the Centre launched vocational qualifications courses for CNC machine operators. The curriculum was developed in close co-operation with local employers working in the metallurgy sector. The entire course lasted over 1200 hours (approximately one year), and completion of the course increased chances of obtaining a job in the sector. Thus, the courses are popular and the number of candidates exceeds the number of available placements. The weakness is that the course is organised only once a year – it starts in September and lasts 39 weeks, which makes it more difficult to adjust to the needs of students. The centre is able to provide more courses, but it would require additional financial resources (the courses are financed by the state budget) and more flexible organisation of the courses.

The curriculum of the course is modular and certified by the Polish Network of Modular Education (the certifying body for modular and vocational education).

approach within the framework of a project entitled "Time for Professionals", financed by the European Social Fund (see Box 3.8). As a result of these efforts, modular education has become ever more popular in vocational education for youth and adults (however, comprehensive data on actual usage is not currently available).

Assessment of the accessibility of training and education should also take into account organisational flexibility and opportunities for combining education with work or personal obligations. Some insights are provided by a recent study by the Central Statistical Office on adult learning. In this context, it is important to distinguish adult education, undertaken mostly in the form of formal education (higher education, colleges and post-secondary education, and schools for adults) and non-formal education (undertaken in the form of courses, training, and workshops and usually provided by private companies).[2] In 2011, 5.4% of the adult population (25-64 years old) participated in formal education and 21% participated in non-formal education. Participation in formal education is usually initiated and financed by the students themselves. In this context, it is important to ensure the possibility of combining education with other activities, and a significant part of this education is organised in the evenings and during weekends. Non-formal education tends to be organised during working hours or in close liaison with the workplace (CSO, 2013a) and over 70% of cases are financed or co-financed by employers. The majority of institutions that offer education or training adjust to these trends, and the available research does not report significant barriers related to the organisation of training and education.

The real challenge is still the quality of education and training, especially in regards to non-formal education. The quality of the formal education is regulated by the state through a number of instruments. The National Qualification Framework (NQF) was recently established and incorporates formal education. Non-formal education is less regulated and is not covered by the NQF but in some cases, the quality of training is assured by national or sectorial regulations. The Ministry of Education is working on a new law on the National System of Qualification, which will be based on the NQF and will consist of a national qualifications register and mechanisms to ensure the quality of qualifications.

Another instrument for ensuring the quality of educational services is the Register of Development Services, which is produced by the Polish Agency of Enterprise Development. This instrument is combined with a new mechanism for distributing the European Social Fund for training. To date, the distribution of resources has been based on the supply side, namely training companies applying for ESF financing and then recruiting employers and employees for the training programme. The new mechanism will be more demand driven – employers will be entitled to apply directly for training vouchers, with which they can co-finance training and other development services according to their needs.

Access to training through the public employment services

In Poland, the development of the skills and competences of unemployed persons is an important element of active labour market policies. Training for the unemployed and job-seekers is mostly provided by poviat labour offices, but the scale of this policy intervention depends heavily on available resources and the preferences of poviat labour offices regarding the allocation of resources between different instruments. In recent years, poviat labour offices have spent around 4-5% of total spending for active labour market policies on training addressed to the unemployed. This is a significant change in comparison to the situation in 2006-08, when local offices spent an average of 9% of all resources on active labour market policies on training (Figure 3.12).

Figure 3.12. **Spending on training as a percentage of all spending on active labour market policies, Poland, 2006-15**

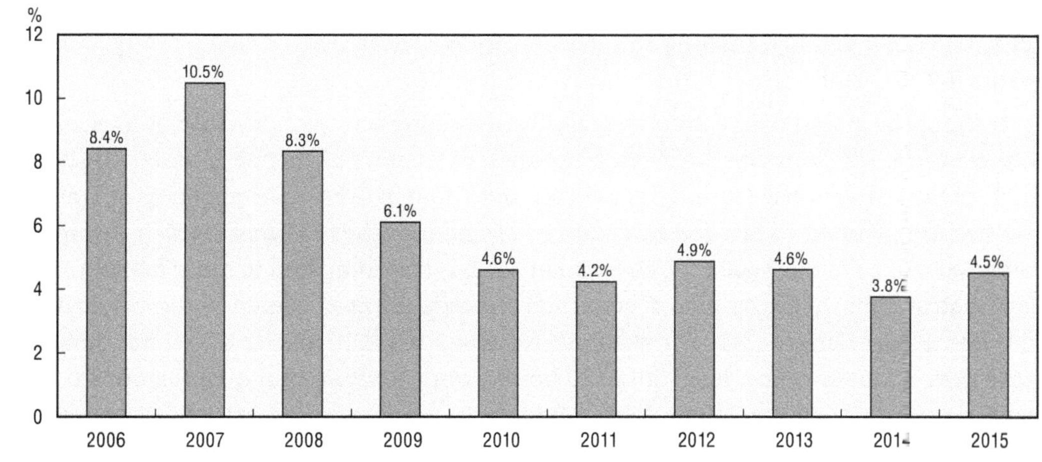

Source: MLSP (2015a), *Detailed information on Labour Fund spending between 2006-2014 and plans for 2015.*

The decrease in spending on training activities, combined with the overall reduction of resources of the Labour Fund in 2011 and the increase in the number of unemployed persons, led to a sharp decline in the percentage of the unemployed participating in training, from 11% in 2008 to almost 4% in 2013. The sharpest decline was observed between 2010 and 2011. This may have been caused by the reductions in the Labour Fund. The level of participation of unemployed in training may differ between poviat labour offices. In 2014 about 8% of registered unemployed persons participated in subsidised training in Poznań, while this figure was only about 3% in Radom.

Figure 3.13. **Percentage of unemployed persons participating in training, Poland, 2004-13**

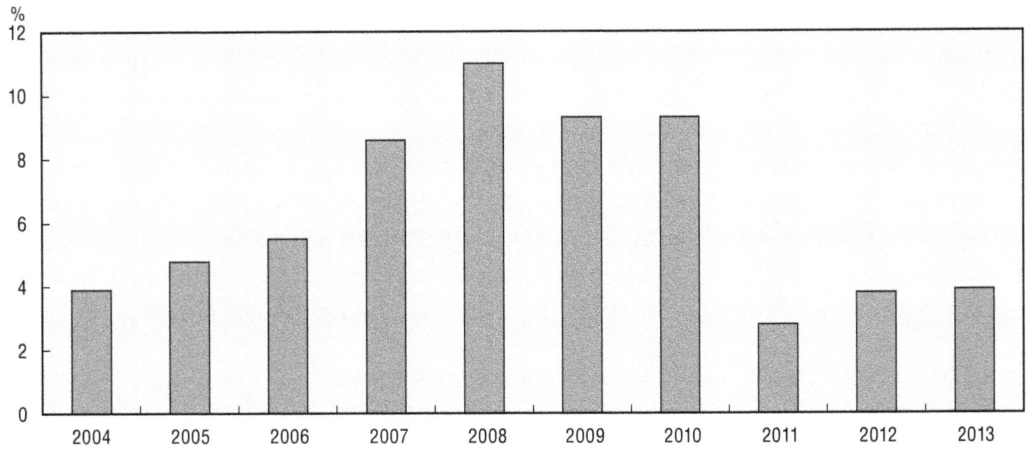

Source: MLSP (2014b),*Training and practice and other forms of developing the qualifications of the unemployed*, Ministry of Labour and Social Policy, Warsaw.

The training provided by poviat labour offices can be organised in two basic ways:

- Group training – poviat labour offices commission training for a group of unemployed persons and then starts the recruitment process,
- Individual training – poviat labour offices commission training adjusted to the needs of an individual unemployed person. This can be initiated by the unemployed person, if he/she justifies the probability of gaining employment. This type of training can also be organised on the basis of a tripartite agreement (between the poviat labour office, employer and unemployed person). In 2013, about one-third of all training activities were organised as individual training and this percentage has increased significantly in recent years (MLSP, 2014b).

It should be stressed here that the majority of training activities provided by local offices are short term. For example, the average duration of training in Poznań is under 104 hours, which means that most training is shorter than four weeks. The majority of training activities are planned to last for a maximum of one month (150 hours) which means the average cost of training (2 400 PLN, 600 Euro in 2013) is low compared to other labour market policy instruments. In the opinion of some stakeholders, courses offered by the employment office do not last long enough. For example, training for a CNC machine operator, financed by the poviat labour office, lasts only 150 hours, while a vocational qualifications course provided by the Centre for Practical Education in the same city lasts over 1 200 hours. The poviat labour office in Radom does not use the capacity of the Centre as a training provider, preferring shorter and cheaper forms of education provided most often by private companies. This is a common trend – local institutions specialised in vocational education provide a limited number of training activities for the unemployed.

It should be noted that recent amendments to the Law on the promotion of employment increased the number of instruments that support education and training. A new form of providing training is the training voucher, addressed to unemployed persons under the age of 30. An unemployed person that receives a voucher may autonomously select the most appropriate training on the market, up to a threshold set by the poviat labour office. According to representatives of the poviat labour office, these instruments positively increase the autonomy of unemployed persons, their engagement and responsibility for the success of the entire activation process.

Another new instrument implemented by poviat labour offices to support the training of adult employed persons is the National Training Fund. The logic of this instrument is rather simple: micro and small enterprises can apply to poviat labour offices for reimbursements of 80% to 100% of the cost of training. In 2015, support was limited to employees above 45 years of age. This approach addresses an above-mentioned market failure: employers, especially of smaller enterprises, are less interested in investing in the skills of older workers and thus public incentives may, at least to some extent, improve the situation. 2014 was treated as a pilot year of the new instrument and available funds were limited (0.4% of Labour Fund resources devoted to this active labour market policy). In 2015, available resources were significantly increased to 3%. Poviat labour offices also noticed considerable interest in this measure on the part of employers.

The new instrument is currently being evaluated, and it is too early to assess its effectiveness. According to respondents, the new instrument is popular among small and medium enterprises, showing that it answers the needs of some employers and employees. However, the poviat labour offices generally do not have enough capacity to ensure value for money of the subsidised trainings, especially in the context of the lack of a national qualifications system that encompasses non-formal education and the certification of the training. There is also a lack of data on the characteristics of employers that use this instrument. The new instrument does not seem to address one of the main weaknesses of small enterprises: low capacity in the area of human resources management. Micro and small enterprises often have difficulties in identifying the training needs of their employees and planning their development. The National Training Fund may finance the identification of enterprises' skills needs and the planning of skills development, but respondents note that the support is limited to training in most cases.

The main instrument for training employees is the European Social Fund. Between 2008 and 2014, over one million adult employed persons participated in training provided through projects financed by the ESF, coordinated by PES, NGOs and private companies. And although the number is high, the yearly average was slightly under 130 000 persons. 16% of participants were persons over 50 years of age and 33% were persons with low qualifications. This helps to ameliorate the fact that groups in relatively better situations (better educated; younger; living in larger cities /urban areas; employed; and/or working in larger companies) have higher rates of participation. However, the scale of support for older workers and those with lower qualifications is still insufficient.

Other institutions may also provide training and other forms of improving the competences of unemployed persons, especially local NGOs and training companies, with projects financed by other sources (e.g. the European Social Fund). In both studied areas, a number of such projects were identified; however, there was a lack of data to assess the scope of these activities.

Training in basic and generic skills

Available data clearly show that a need for basic skills provision exists. According to PIAAC research (The Programme for the International Assessment of Adult Competencies), coordinated by OECD and conducted in Poland by the Educational Research Institute, 19% of adults in Poland have literacy skills at level 1 or below (compared to 15% in OECD countries) and 24% of adults in Poland have numeracy skills at level 1 or below (compared to 19% in OECD countries) (OECD, 2014a). Low levels of literacy or numeracy are more common among older persons, men, and residents of rural areas, whereas training in basic skills is more popular among younger adults who had problems finishing school. It should also be mentioned that almost 70% of those persons have completed some level of secondary education.

Basic skills training generally receives limited attention amongst the training provided by public institutions. There are a few institutions offering courses for adults at the primary and lower secondary education level; however, these courses are usually long and the number of participants is rather low. There are no short term courses to improve numeracy or literacy skills for adults (IER, 2013). Public employment services do not offer this type of support and tend to focus instead on the improvement of vocational skills. In practice, the scope of this type of support is very limited, provided occasionally and in an informal way.

Higher-level generic skills are one of the key elements of the core curriculum for vocational education, and usually the development of these types of skills is a part of vocational education and courses, both for youth and adults. Monitoring of the implementation of the new core curriculum shows that the vast majority of schools include these topics as part of other classes and do not organise separate classes or courses for the development of basic skills (NCSVET, 2015). A key challenge is that teachers are often not properly prepared to teach such skills and most of them declare that they do not need training in this field.

Work-based training and apprenticeships

According to employers, one of the main weaknesses of job candidates is the lack of professional experience and skills necessary to function in the work place. This problem is particularly evident in the case of youth completing their education and entering the labour market. As a result, there has been a strong emphasis on increasing the scale and improving the quality of work-based training offered by the public sector. Improving the quality of vocational education is one of the priorities of the European Social Fund for the period of 2014-20. Regional authorities that manage ESF attach great importance to work-based learning and the co-operation of vocational schools with employers.

According to the Polish law on the education system, all VET students should participate in practical training. The scale and type of work-based education depends on the type of school. Technical upper secondary schools offer a four-week placement, which supports the learning process. In basic vocational schools, at least 60% of the time spent in education should be work-based learning.

Work based education in initial VET can be organised in the following ways: workshops in VET schools, centres for practical education/centres for continuous education, enterprises, and farms. Another important mechanism of work-based training is apprenticeships. In this type of training, students work 2-3 days a week in an enterprise on the basis of a labour contract, with the remaining time spent in vocational school to develop general skills. If students pass the vocational exam, the employer is financially rewarded for the education provided. Apprenticeships are acknowledged as a particularly effective mechanism of vocational education. The major segment of this type of education is found in craft enterprises. All craft enterprises are federated in regional craft chambers and the national Polish Craft Association. The structure takes responsibility for the quality of work-based education in the craft enterprises. This form of learning has a particularly strong tradition in Wielkopolska, where almost 12 000 participated in this type of work-based education in 2014. This is almost 16% of the total participants in work-based education in Poland's craft enterprises. Another important institution for work-based training is the Voluntary Labour Corps (see textbox below). The "Time for Professionals" programme in in the Wielkoposka Region is another promising approach.

Box 3.7. **Voluntary Labour Corps**

The Voluntary Labour Corps is a labour market institution, which also conducts educational activities. The main target group for the organisation is youth, 15-18 years old, at risk of dropping out from the educational system. One of the main areas of activity is vocational education, provided in the form of work-based education. The work-based education takes place in craft enterprises or in the workshops of the Labour Corps. Practical education is combined with general education at a primary, lower secondary or basic vocational school. The Voluntary Labour Corps manages the whole process, providing:

- assistance with the selection of a profession (individualised vocational counselling);
- assistance with the identification of an appropriate enterprise, negotiating the agreement and conditions of work and education;
- assistance with the selection an appropriate school; and
- additional courses and lessons.

The Voluntary Labour Corps also provides additional services to both the adolescent and his/her family. Each participant is under the supervision of a tutor, who monitors progress in education, work conditions, organises psychological and pedagogical support, provides additional lessons in case problems arise with the educational process. If needed, participants can also live in a dormitory. The services of the Labour Corps are comprehensive, based on years of experience. Its activities are financed by the Labour Fund, state budget and also the European Social Fund.

Box 3.8. **"Time for Professionals"**

Another project being implemented by regional authorities and Poznań University of Technology is "Time for professionals", whose main objective is to improve the quality of VET in the Wielkoposka Region, including through enhancing work-based learning. There are a number of activities in the project, however, two are most important here:

- Laboratories – which are well equipped facilities for work-based learning. The equipment standards found here to prepare students for their future work exceed what is typically found in enterprises. The laboratories provide week long, work-based training for groups of students from schools from the whole region.
- Support for the development of work-based learning in enterprises – the main effort of the project is to facilitate better co-operation between schools and employers. The project promotes co-operation with employers and vocational schools in the field of practical learning: improved communication, improved organisation of work-based learning and making it more flexible in order to better adjust to the situation of employers.

While, there is a lack of national data on the structure of work-based education, some studies and estimates are available. According to research conducted by the Mazowiecki Observatory of the Labour Market, an average of 37% of VET students in the Radomski sub-region participated in work-based training organised in enterprises in 2011, which is below average (41%) for the entire region . There is a lack of data concerning apprenticeships in VET in Poznań and the Wielkopolska Region (MLMO, 2011b)

Finally, for those who already have left the education system and are still experiencing difficulties on the labour market, there are instruments that enable them to acquire work experience provided by poviat labour offices. The most popular is work placement, which allows participants to gain professional experience as well as professional skills, and thus can be treated as training on the job. In 2013, about 27% of all resources for active labour market policies was spent on this instrument (MLSP, 2014b) and about 42% of all unemployed persons participating in activation measures took part in this form of training (comparing to 18% in formal and non-formal training programmes). Unemployed young adults (up to 30 years old) can apply for a work placement voucher, which allows them to independently select an enterprise in which they wish to be placed (provided that the employer guarantees employment after the work placement period).

Working with employers on training

The Balance of Human Capital study, conducted every year for five years, provides solid insight about the expectations of employers. Generally, a significant majority of employers report problems with the recruitment of new employees. In 2014, 80% of all employers seeking new workers experienced some difficulties. Problems were more often reported by small enterprises and in sectors such as construction, transport, care and health services. In identifying the source of recruitment difficulties, employers most frequently indicated that applicant candidates did not meet their expectations (two-thirds of the problems cited). The key problem was the shortage of candidates with the required skills. Every year, one-third of employers experiencing difficulties in finding suitable workers identified this as a challenge. The second most often cited problem was the lack of appropriate professional experience. Employers distinguished three main groups of required skills:

- Professional – named by almost 60% of employers seeking employees and experiencing difficulties in finding them;
- Self-organisation – more than one-quarter of employers declared that they experienced difficulties in finding independent, entrepreneurial, stress-resistant candidates; and
- Interpersonal – one-tenth of employers found it difficult to find candidates with adequate levels of communication skills, and group work skills (Kocór et al., 2015).

Taking this all into account, it is not surprising that employers report that training curricula are not aligned to their needs and demands. In terms of VET curricula, the most critical problems identified include the following:

- Out-of-date curricula – the majority of schools do not co-operate with employers in developing their curriculum, have limited contacts with the labour market and offer training that is not adjusted to changing technologies in the sectors.
- Curricula that are overloaded with theoretical, abstract knowledge which has been assessed by employers as not useful in the workplace.

- Weak links between theoretical and practical learning in VET – these are often two separate paths of training and lack integration and co-ordination.
- Inadequate competences of VET teachers – in many cases, their knowledge is out-dated and they lack professional experience from the industry. This complaint was most often cited in relation to teachers responsible for practical learning.
- Out-dated equipment for vocational education in schools – workshops for practical learning are, in the opinion of employers, drastically underinvested. Paradoxically, students in schools that lack workshops for practical education are in a better situation because schools organise practical education in enterprises or in better equipped centres for practical education.
- Not enough practical learning – from the employers' point of view, practical learning is the most important element of education and in their opinion, the duration of this training is inadequate. This relates particularly to technical schools (ISCED 3c level), where practical learning lasts only 4-6 weeks per year.
- The low quality of workplace learning organised in enterprises and the inadequate supervision of this by schools.
- Inadequate competences of graduates – employers complain that some students that have completed school and vocational exams present a very low level of practical competences in the work place (for example, hairdressers) (MLMO, 2012).

Despite the difficulties associated with finding employees and complaints about the quality of vocational education, few employers work together with vocational schools. The OECD study visit identified several reasons for this. One of these was that VET institutions usually operate with a language based on the core curriculum, while employers use a more practical and everyday language to describe their needs. Additionally, VET providers have difficulties translating employers' expectations into practice in the education and training process, and employers are resistant to devoting their time and effort to work with VET institutions.

Another significant problem identified during this study was the lack of any intermediary mechanisms facilitating collaboration between VET institutions and local employers. As such, there is no systematic mechanism for collecting information on the needs of local employers, providing this information to VET institutions, and supporting VET institutions in adjusting their educational programmes to the needs of local employers.

Several examples of employers initiating new courses or occupations were identified. However, schools did not always accept their proposals, mostly due to financial or formal limitations. In practice, most VET institutions do not work closely with employers. Survey results from Wielkopolska in 2014 show that only about 10% of VET institutions declared that employers have a real impact on the scope of education and on the curriculum and only 8% declared that employers actively participated in designing their curriculum (e.g. participated in the school board) (ROLMW, 2014). This number clearly indicates that there is much room for improvement.[3]

Despite this, there are a number of examples of collaboration between VET institutions and employers. For example, the metallurgy sector in Radom is one of the most important business sectors in the city. Employers representing the sector raised the problem of the inadequate number of graduates prepared for work in their companies and decided to support VET education (see previous Box 3.6). The City of Poznań, as the authority responsible for VET and adult training, has undertaken several initiatives to help better adjust the VET offer to the needs of the local labour market:

- Establishing the Observatory of the Economy and Labour Market for the Poznań Agglomeration – to provide data on current and future labour market needs,
- Developing a network of Sector Centres of VET in Wielkopolska – the centres will provide high quality vocational education in the sectors important to the local economy.

Matching people to jobs and facilitating progression

Activation and job-matching through PES

Job matching is a key task of the poviat labour office. Evidence suggests that employers use poviat labour offices when looking for low-skilled employees, while employers looking for high and medium skilled employees use other recruitment channels. In 2014, Poznań's poviat labour office registered over 15 500 jobs offers (compared to 10 500 jobs offers in 2013) (PLOP, 2015). The structure of job offers in Poznań in 2014 was as follows:

- 6% required the completion of higher education;
- 22% required the completion of upper secondary education;
- 37% required the completion of vocational education (both upper secondary and basic); and
- 35% had no requirements for qualifications.

This can be compared to the structure of job vacancies in the general economy, which is provided by the Central Statistical Office. The CSO only provides information for a large group of occupations; however, some conclusions can be formulated based on this data. As shown in the table below, 26% of all job offers are for managers and professionals, mostly with higher education, 45% are for persons with VET education, while only 6% of job offers in the economy are for basic occupations – mostly for persons without an education.

Table 3.1. **Average number of job offers by occupation, Poland, 2014**

	Total	Managers	Professionals	Technicians and associate professionals	Clerical support workers	Craft and related trades workers	Plant and machine operators and assemblers	Elementary occupations
In thousands	54.4	2.1	11.7	4.8	6.0	11.2	8.4	3.5
Percentage	100%	4%	22%	9%	11%	21%	15%	6%

Note: The study collected the data on the number of job offers at the end of each quarter. The average for one year is the average for the date of the status at the end of each quarter.
Source: CSO (2015), Demand for labour, Central Statistical Office, Warsaw.

According to the Law on the promotion of employment, each job offer may be registered only once in a single employment office, which can then inform other offices about the offer. In the analysed employment offices, there are on-line job matching services available on a web page. For example, in Poznań's local office, job postings are up to date, but only for the local labour market. The service enables a user to search for job offers only by territory.

Assessing the effectiveness of activation through the public employment services is made difficult by the fact that there is a lack of information on the percentage of unemployed persons that receive professional job counselling within the first 30 days after registration and the percentage of unemployed persons that receive training or a job offer within the first few months of their unemployment claim. However, what is known is that access to labour market services and instruments depends heavily on the availability of resources, as well as the situation of the unemployed person. The mechanism of profiling, described earlier, resulted in the lack of access to such instruments by unemployed persons categorised to the third profile. In August 2015, this was almost one-third of all registered unemployed persons.

However, the new client advisor position in the employment office could significantly improve this situation. Services of the client advisor include meeting with the unemployed person to discuss and assess his/her skills and expectations, and on this basis, preparing a plan of activation measures to be undertaken. The unemployed persons who have problems specifying their career plans or do not have well-prepared job application documents are directed to individual visits with vocational counsellors.

Career guidance and planning

In the course of the study, most respondents pointed to the need to develop and strengthen career guidance in schools, especially at the lower secondary level (before students choose VET or general education). This was also highlighted as a challenge in the OECD's 2016 Economic Survey of Poland (OECD, 2016a). Under current law, schools are required to provide professional counselling. They may hire a vocational advisor for this purpose or delegate this task to another employee, such as a pedagogue or another teacher who should receive relevant training. However, respondents pointed out that current career support is insufficient and very often of low quality.

For example, typical problems with counselling in schools are presented in a recent study on career planning support in the Mazowiecki Region for the Radomski sub-region (MLMO, 2013). A vast majority of schools (80-90%) declared that they provide some kind of career planning support. This task is done by a teacher in 57% of schools, and by a pedagogue in 35% of schools. In the Radomski sub-region, about 70% of persons have attained a formal qualification for performing this task (which is much higher than the average for the region). 70% of schools co-operate with other institutions, and co-operation with the Youth Career Centres and Mobile Centres for Vocational Information is generally positively assessed (both institutions are part of the Voluntary Labour Corps). While students generally assess career support positively, they also note that support is sometimes provided in an unattractive manner. Additionally, an in-depth qualitative study provided a rather negative assessment of the quality of career planning support, identifying the following key problems: persons responsible for this task are often not properly trained; inadequate time is spent on this type of support; funds are lacking for these services; the services provided are of low quality; and the services provided are inadequate.

The research clearly shows that the legal obligation of schools to provide vocational counselling is insufficient to secure good quality counselling at an adequate scale. The basic source of information for students is still their friends and relatives, thus in many cases, their decisions are made on an intuitive basis. One solution is Career School Centres, which are organisational units responsible for vocational counselling. However, this type of service exists in only about 9% of schools in the Mazowiecki Region.

Career planning services for youth are also provided by other institutions:

- The Voluntary Labour Corps (described earlier) established a network of over 500 units providing professional counselling including Mobile Centres of Vocational Information, Youth Centres of Education and Work, Youth Career Centres, Youth job offices, and Job matching services (employment agencies).
- Poviat labour offices co-operate with schools (counsellors from offices visit schools, and organise meetings with employers), and also provide direct services for unemployed youth.
- Psychological-Pedagogical Centres operate on the county level, providing mostly psychological and pedagogical support; however, to some extent they also provide vocational counselling services.
- Regional labour offices provide career support services for all interested persons, including youth.

Local authorities can also have significant impact on access and the quality of job counselling services. In Poznań, for example, the city established a Centre for Professional Counselling for Youth. This institution provides support to schools (workshops for small groups of students in schools, individual consultations for students, support for persons working as career advisers in schools). This is an example of supporting schools to provide job counselling to their students at the local level. However, evidence is lacking to be able to determine the extent to which this activity is sufficient.

Adults can also benefit from career guidance and planning. One segment of career guidance services for adults is the career offices that exist at most higher education institution. They usually provide services such as:

- Developing the skills related to searching for a job (training, counselling, workshops);
- Organising professional practice at local enterprises;
- Meeting with employers (career fairs, sector meetings); and
- Presenting job offers to students and graduates.

Career office staff usually work closely with local employers (invite them to fairs, present job prospects, etc.). In Wielkopolska, career offices established a network and are working together to improve their own skills.

Providing career guidance and planning is also one of the tasks of employment offices. Poviat labour offices provide these services to unemployed persons and job seekers, using job counsellors. In recent years, the number of professional job counsellors in local offices has significantly increased; however, their number is still low. In 2014, there were 863 unemployed persons for each job counsellor, while in 2005, this number was 4 616 – over five times higher. In practice, however, only some of the unemployed may have been served. For example, in 2014, job counsellors in Poznań provided support to about 1 200 persons in the form of individual support and about 600 in the form of group support, which correspond to 12% of the registered unemployed (PLOP, 2015). In the Radomski sub-region, around 10 000 persons received career support services, a further 18 000 received individual support, which corresponds to 9% of the registered unemployed (VLO, 2015). Additionally, in 2014, a new job position was introduced: client advisor. The main objective of this position is to ensure an individualised approach to working with clients.

Regional employment offices also provide career planning support for all interested adults. Such a centre also operates in Radom, providing a broad range of services (individual advice, group counselling, and identification of skills). However, the most common type of service is the provision of more general vocational information.

Facilitating progression for low skilled workers

An evident gap in the system of adjusting competences to meet the needs of employers is the lack of comprehensive policies for workers with low qualifications. Although this group is often mentioned as one of the target groups in strategies and programmes, there are no specific actions addressed to this group. While workers with low qualifications are eligible to use the available services of local and regional employment offices, in practice they use such services rather rarely. A study conducted in 2009 showed that only 3% of low-skilled workers have ever used career development support and only 25% expressed interest in doing so, while 7% stated that they would surely do so. Persons from this group are not aware of the benefits of such services, lack knowledge about career support (what it is, the types of benefits it can bring, etc.), and they approach it with a high degree of mistrust (PAED, 2009). Poviat labour offices prefer to invest in the skills of better educated unemployed persons because of their higher probability of success.

Mapping job profiles

In Poland, there is a lack of reliable outlines of the skills and competences required for jobs in specific sectors. In fact, no institution exists that could conduct such analyses at the national level. Regional observatories of the labour market, financed by the European Social Fund, try to fill this gap. However, their reports are based on different methodological approaches, conducted at different levels (e.g. the whole region, specific sectors). In some cases, the quality of the research is also rather poor or too general. Therefore, there is also a lack of evidence that such reports are widely used by local actors. The situation at the national level may improve in future years through the upcoming establishment of Sectoral Skills Councils, which will be set up by the Polish Agency of Enterprise Development.

Joined up approaches to skills

Retaining and attracting skilled workers is also a key component of economic development efforts. Attracting talent is one of the priorities for local authorities in both study areas. However, the situation in each sub-region differs significantly. Radom and its whole sub-region have experienced a net negative migration. Many persons migrated to Warsaw or abroad. Therefore, local authorities are considering activities to encourage people to stay in Radom or return from other cities. However, specific activities are still in the planning stage, rather than actually being implemented.

Poznań, with a much larger labour market and a strong academic centre, is also interested in attracting talent. Local authorities are also aware that attracting talent is key to improving the competitiveness of local and regional businesses. In a number of documents, as well as in the "Strategy of the City of Poznań", the need to attract talent is emphasised. In most cases, these strategies and actions focus on attracting new students rather than more experienced professionals. This strategy is based on the assumption that mobility in Poland is relatively low and, in fact, students are the most mobile segment of society. Therefore, the city finances grants and scholarships for talented students as an incentive for them to study in Poznań. There is also strong pressure to improve the labour market situation, especially to attract investors in high tech and other high-skilled sectors, which offer attractive jobs.

Theme 3: Targeting policy to local employment sectors and investing in quality jobs

Figure 3.14. **Dashboard results: Targeting policy to local employment sectors and investing in quality jobs**

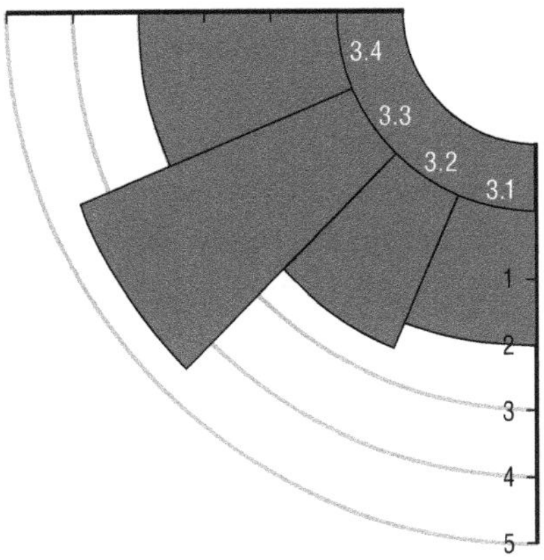

Relevance of provision of policies to important local employment sectors, global trends and challenges

Relevance to important local employment sectors

Local stakeholders are paying more attention to the actual needs of the local labour market. 67% of respondents amongst surveyed poviat labour offices reported that "generally, training is geared towards employer demand but improvements could still be made."

Table 3.2. **Extent to which training available locally (e.g. through PES, post-secondary schools and colleges) meets employer needs/demand for skilled workers**

	Percent of respondents
No efforts are made to align training with local employer needs	1.0
Some efforts are made, but employers report significant problems with training not being aligned to their needs	3.4
Generally, training is geared towards meeting employer demand but improvements could still be made	67.3
Training is very well-aligned with the needs of employers	28.4

Source: 2015 OECD LEED survey to poviat labour offices.

Local stakeholders are also increasingly aware that their programmes should not be addressed to general "labour market needs", but should focus instead on particular sectors and branches. However, in order to address these issues, solid and reliable analysis is needed that includes the local as well as sectoral dimension. Without such knowledge, local actors plan their employment programmes on the basis of their knowledge, opinions and intuition or – in many cases – on the basis of previous experience (i.e. path dependency), which may be misleading.

Regional authorities are attempting to fill this knowledge gap by establishing Regional Observatories of the Labour Market. In recent years, the Observatory for Wielkopolska conducted the following analyses:

- *The importance of SMEs for the development of Wielkopolska;*
- *Conditions for the development of industrial processing in Wielkopolska;*
- *Prospects for trade in Wielkopolska;* and
- *The present and future of the construction sector in Wielkopolska.*

A similar situation can be observed in the Mazowiecki Region, where the Regional Observatory of the Labour Market published a study called *The demand for qualifications and competences on the Mazowieckie regional labour market* which presents the needs of particular sectors and sub-regional labour markets.

Unfortunately, evidence collected over the course of the study suggest that local stakeholders do not use the reports prepared for the regional level, although they are aware that such reports are prepared and distributed. The conclusions and recommendations of these analyses are often fairly general, limiting their usefulness for and influence on practitioners and policy makers (especially at the local level). More detailed analysis is needed at the level of sectors or sub-regional labour markets, and more effort should be made to integrate the findings from these studies into employment programmes in practice.

In practice, it is employers representing larger, international enterprises that initiate a significant proportion of employment or educational initiatives geared towards the current and future needs of the local labour market. This is the case of Volkswagen in Wielkopolska, which co-operates very closely with several VET institutions in order to ensure the adequate education of their future staff. Another example is Solaris, a Polish company specialising in the production of buses.

Smaller enterprises are less active in forecasting their future needs and less interested in undertaking co-operation with local authorities, poviat labour offices or VET institutions in order to ensure a supply of capable employees. The evidence for this can be seen in the relatively small proportion of training financed by poviat labour offices on the basis of the tripartite agreement and the low number of employers co-operating with VET institutions. At the same time, most employers declare that they encounter problems in securing adequately skilled workers (Kocór et al., 2015).

There are other examples of coordinated approaches to addressing skills gaps at the local level. A positive example of a joint strategy for skills development has been identified in business-to-business services, a rapidly developing sector in Poland that has a very high potential for growth. In Poznań, a local partnership was established between a local university, business centre and municipal companies to establish a postgraduate study programme entitled *Modern business services*.

Another example is the above-mentioned metallurgy sector in the Radomski sub-region that experienced a lack of skilled graduates. As a result, representatives of enterprises in this sector developed a strategy to resolve this problem in close co-operation with local authorities and several schools. Their main activities were:

- Producing a film for students to present the character of the work in the metallurgy sector in order to counter negative stereotypes about work in this sector;
- Financing a set of textbooks and workbooks for new students;

- Organising apprenticeships for students; and
- Offering jobs to graduates.

This year, the first cohort will graduate and start work in the industry. While representatives of the Radomski sub-region noted that this strategy was successful, on the other hand, some other local stakeholders noted that the strategy should have been developed and actions undertaken before the skill gap occurred.

Local and regional actors usually have to take into consideration a number of factors, at times contradictory, when planning the offer of vocational education and training and adapting it to local needs. For example, directors of schools, but also in some cases local authorities, often treat the supply of education and training services (existing infrastructure, equipment, qualifications and profiles of teachers, local traditions of VET) as key to determining the occupations being offered. As schools are often major employers in the local labour market of some smaller counties, efforts to adjust offerings can be met with resistance. Additionally, employer and student demand for VET services are not always compatible. While employers may look to VET to train for particular occupations, as well as for specific competences, student preferences are not always in line with these demands. Additionally, students often perceive VET as low prestige and offering poor quality jobs.

These factors may sometimes push in opposite directions. For example, local authorities in Radom decided to start new classes and offer new occupations according to the needs of local employers. Unfortunately, the experiment was unsuccessful because very few new students applied to attend this training. On the other hand, Radom also has a positive example of responding to local labour market demands in the metallurgy sector described earlier.

Relevance of global trends

In terms of taking into account larger, global trends and their impact on the labour market, there are examples of regional analyses that focus on new trends in technology. For example, the Regional Observatory in the Mazowiecki Region implements a project titled *Development Trends for Mazowsze*. The project provides a number of in-depth studies on the development of the region. However, they lack an analysis of the impact of global trends on the regional and local labour markets.

Local labour market institutions present a rather low level of engagement in analysis that forecasts and manages needs for the skills of a green economy or care services. For example, in the identified examples, the development of a green economy and the care sector is not mentioned. This overall gap may be due to not understanding the significance of these processes (OECD, 2011). On the other hand, interviewed participants note that this approach may result from the low priority attached to employment in the green economy by the national authorities responsible for the labour market.

Despite the lack of attention at the local level, recent analysis of the needs of employers shows that the health and care sectors are among those with higher percentages of employers reporting difficulties in filling job vacancies (Kocór et al., 2015). Also, numerous studies point out the need for developing care and health services. A recent study also shows that the number of jobs in the green economy in Poland in 2012 was 34 000, significantly lower than in other EU countries, such as Germany or France (EurObser'ER, 2013). Forecasts show that the number of jobs could be increased by 100 000, but this largely depends on the policies and regulations adopted by Polish authorities.

While there are overall gaps in attention paid to these global labour market trends, there are also good examples of education authorities that recognise the importance of both sectors particularly the green economy. In Radom, activities have been initiated by the Institute for Sustainable Technologies, an active and acknowledged institution in the area of vocational education and training. The Institute, in co-operation with a local public vocational training institution, the poviat labour office and partners from France, implemented a project whose main objective was to develop a new occupation of waste and recycling operator, as well as to develop and implement modular training for this occupation. The main backdrop for this project was the development of a green economy and the growing need for trained professionals in this sector. The Institute is currently developing additional approaches and projects in this area, emphasising the need for thinking ahead.

Also, other VET intuitions in Poland are becoming more interested in the green economy, as have higher education institutions. Over the past three to five years, several of them have initiated courses in the field of "the green economy". Additionally, this topic is being further developed in a number of faculties (Sudak, 2015). This development clearly shows an improvement in the situation compared to 2011, when an OECD study concluded that opportunities for formal education in this sector are very rare in Poland (OECD, 2011).

Work with employers on skills utilisation and productivity

Improving work organisation and productivity improvements

Local, regional and national actors declare that they are aware of the importance of skills utilisation and work organisation for improving the competitiveness of companies. A recent study on the barriers to the growth of Polish enterprises found that the most important factors preventing growth are internal: lack of good managers; lack of the delegation of tasks; poor organisation of work; low teamwork competences'; lack of planning; and the domination of ad-hoc actions (PAED, 2014).

The Polish Agency for Enterprise Development is particularly active in this field. The Agency conducted several studies and on this basis has been implementing a number of activities. Some examples are:

- Strategic planning in micro, small and medium enterprises – a pilot project supporting 80 enterprises in developing and implementing strategies for growth. Important elements of these strategies were the development of skills and skills utilisation.
- National system of services for enterprises – a nationwide network of institutions supporting businesses. The services provided by the institutions are mostly financed by European funds, distributed by PAED, which is also responsible for the quality assurance of the services. Although the network also supports skills utilisation and work organisation, the main types of services include: sources of financing, establishment of new enterprises, and legal aspects of economic activity. Employers are less interested in the "soft" aspects of management (MRD, 2012).

The "harder" aspects of business dominate in the support services offered to enterprises, and references to "soft" management skills also seem to be missing at the local level in both study areas. For example, the Poznań Centre for Entrepreneurship Support does not offer services related to work organisation and skills utilisation. Its offer is more focused on such topics as taxes, legal issues, marketing, and new technologies. Within local PES offices, only 31% of respondents to the OECD survey reported that they work with local employers to improve human resource/workplace organisation management.

Due to the small scale of activities or the low interest in skills utilisation and work organisation, there is significant room to improve the situation. A new mechanism developed by PAED in co-operation with employers known as the Register of Development Services may bring some improvement. The main idea of this Register is to develop a new, demand driven system of supporting the development of skills in enterprises. The Register records providers of services for enterprises (training, and counselling). In order to be registered, the service provider must fulfil a number of criteria which, according to PAED, should assure the high quality of the services. Unfortunately, the criteria mostly concern the capacity of the service providers (turnover, number of staff, experience), with a lack of criteria related to the quality of the services. Regional authorities will distribute vouchers to enterprises, which can then be used to purchase development services from providers on the Register. This mechanism has not yet been launched.

Sector strategies to improve work organisation or labour productivity were not identified during the research. However, there is evidence that some sectors have a higher-level awareness of the needs for skills development. One example is the sectoral qualifications frameworks that have already been developed for five sectors: banking, IT, telecommunication, sport and tourism. The sectoral qualifications frameworks were developed with the strong engagement of sectoral organisations and associations, who were interested in developing such tools for their branches.

Ensuring the quality of job placements

Another important aspect of ensuring quality jobs is ensuring placements made through the PES are sustainable. As was mentioned earlier, poviat labour offices receive funding according to the number of unemployed persons placed in employment. However, this outcome is calculated after only three months have passed since completion of the activation measures by the unemployed person. While poviat labour offices encourage their staff to ensure the sustainability of job placements, there is a lack of formal incentives and rewards for keeping clients employed over the long-term. Additionally, recently introduced financial rewards for achieving short-term employment outcomes may increase the pressure to achieve immediate employment, potentially at the cost of sustainable employment.

Poviat labour offices do not provide follow-up support for those already placed in employment, even though the initial period of employment is linked with a high risk of failure, especially those who were long-term unemployed. Support for the previously unemployed, but also in some cases for the employer, could significantly increase the rate of sustainable employment. Such an instrument is only available for disabled persons through the National Fund for the Rehabilitation of Disabled Persons.

Promotion of skills for entrepreneurship

Entrepreneurship has been one of the main priorities of Polish national, regional and local authorities for many years. At the heart of the mission of the Polish Agency of Enterprise Development is supporting new enterprises, including small and medium enterprises, and developing an entrepreneurial spirit. Thus, it is not surprising that a number of instruments currently exist to support start-ups and new enterprises, including but not limited to the following:

- Grants for start-ups and assistance with training and counselling, offered by poviat labour offices;

- Grants for start-ups and assistance with training and counselling, financed by the European Social Fund, operated by local and regional providers (in many cases by institutions supporting businesses);
- Support for new enterprises, in the form of grants, counselling, business incubators, financed by the European Regional Fund, also provided by institutions supporting business; and
- Academic Business Incubators, providing support to students and graduates in seeking to establish new enterprises.

There are also examples of local initiatives supporting entrepreneurship. For example, as mentioned earlier, in 1993, Poznań's local authorities established the Centre for Entrepreneurship Support as part of the poviat labour office. The Centre provides support to start-ups (to those who want to establish a new business) as well as to existing enterprises (SMEs). Consequently, the poviat labour office uses the support for start-ups intensively as an instrument of active labour market policy. According to the poviat labour office report 2014, 54% of all funds spent on active labour market policy measures were devoted to supporting entrepreneurship and over 500 persons received grants to establish new businesses (PLOP, 2015).

General data for Poland are more balanced. In 2013, 27% of all resources spent on active labour market policy measures were spent on grants for start-ups, but less than 10% of all activated persons used these grants. The results were similar in 2014. However, overall, Poland spends a higher proportion of its GDP on ALMP start-up incentives than any other OECD country besides the Slovak Republic and Spain (based on 2012 data) (OECD, 2016b).[4] This indicates that although it may be a more resource intensive measure than other ALMP instruments, it is eagerly used by poviat labour offices because the effectiveness of this instrument is perceived to be very high (at least during the first 12 months).

The development of entrepreneurial skills is also an important element of both general and vocational education. As of 2012, Poland was the only country in Europe in which entrepreneurship is an element of the core curriculum at the upper secondary education level and is taught as a required, separate subject (Euridice, 2012). However, stakeholders point out that entrepreneurship education should be more practice oriented, with a stronger emphasis on the development of the skills necessary in the real business world (Kołodziejska, 2012).

Entrepreneurship education and support for start-ups are also important elements of higher education. Entrepreneurship is embedded in the national qualification framework for virtually all fields of study at all levels. However, universities are completely autonomous and are not obligated to include each element of the national qualification framework in their programmes. In practice, entrepreneurship modules are embedded in many subjects. It is also offered as an elective course on occasion, and career offices often offer workshops and seminars to promote entrepreneurship but it is inaccurate to say that they provide most of the elective offerings. An additional option is the offer of academic business incubators. Both local case study areas have such incubators – one in Radom and two in Poznań.

Economic development promotes quality jobs for local people

In recent years, job quality has become a key issue in public discussions of the labour market. Although there is national legislation that secures the basic standards of employment quality (minimum wages, permanent and temporary contracts, labour rights),

Figure 3.15. **Percentage of workers with temporary contracts, Poland in comparison to OECD, 2001-14**

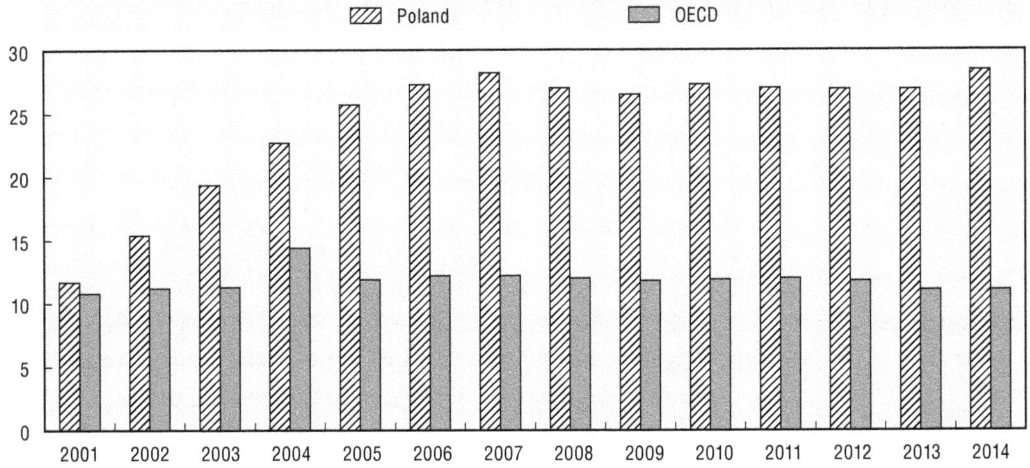

Source: OECD (2016c), "Labour Market Statistics: Employment by permanency of the job", *OECD Employment and Labour Market Statistics* (database), *http://dx.doi.org/10.1787/data-00296-en.*

the recent crisis and the deterioration of the labour market situation have increased pressure on employers to use non-standard, more flexible and less secure types of job contracts more frequently. One measure of this is the percentage of persons working on a temporary basis. As presented in the graph below, the percentage of persons with temporary job contracts is two and a half times higher than the average for OECD countries.

Another specific element of the Polish labour market is the wide usage of civil law contracts for regular employment. The contracts were introduced in Poland in the 1960s in order to enable occasional working. This form of employment is frequently used by employers because the cost of employment is much lower when using such contracts. Employment on the basis of such contracts does not secure many of the labour rights guaranteed by law. It also provides a much lower level of security when a person's employability is interrupted by factors such as pregnancy, disability, and reaching retirement age.

National labour market policies have been focused for many years on creating jobs but their quality has not been a priority. Recently, this approach has been steadily changing, with increasing numbers of economists emphasising the importance of job quality to improve competitiveness and prospects for economic development.

Inward investment strategies focus on skills and quality of jobs

To some extent, the situation at the local level reflects the changes taking place at the national level. In both study areas, local authorities actively seek investors and are aware of the importance of human capital when a new investment is being considered. However, the focus of the strategies of both study areas remains on the number of jobs and, to some extent, their productivity, and less on the quality of the new jobs.

Poznań actively aims to attract investors. Its strategic location (half-way between Warsaw and Berlin), good road and train connections, and skilled labour force all make the city an attractive place for investment. There is a special unit in City Hall whose main task is to co-operate with potential investors and to provide them with all necessary information and support.

Additionally, a number of reports for potential investors are available from the web site of this unit. One of them is about the labour market. It presents information on human capital and wages, but the information is limited to students and graduates with tertiary education and does not mention the level of VET. This is a consequence of the marketing and investment strategy of the city, which focusses on selected sectors including advanced technology, services for business and R&D. A second report focuses on the BPO (business process operation) sector, while another emphasised the number of philology students in Poznań (as foreign language skills may be an important factor for investors in the BPO sector) and the accessibility of office space. Poznań has several important investors in the manufacturing sector including the automotive, food production, pharmaceutical industries. Although these industries require qualified employees with vocational education, and the industry invests heavily in the quality of VET education in the city, it is not mentioned in the reports for investors.

In the strategic documents, local authorities emphasise that their intention is to attract investors in such sectors as IT, where productivity is high, but job creation tends to be low and limited to those who have completed higher education. On the other hand, local authorities also noted that higher wage jobs subsequently increase the demand for services, which usually results in the creation of low paid and unstable jobs. Thus, there are some contradictions in this approach. Unfortunately, there is no evidence of considering the quality of the jobs offered by investors.

In Radom, information for potential investors is easily accessible from the city's web page, including detailed reports for investors that present the local human capital, local educational institutions, the labour market situation, and average wages. Additionally, the city unit responsible for co-operation with investors works with the education unit and is able to provide more detailed information on human capital and education. During the interview, a city representative emphasised that human capital is the second most important condition taken into consideration by potential investors. As Radom has one of the highest unemployment rates in the country, it is standard practice to consider the quantity of jobs to be offered to local residents when making planning decisions in relation to potential local investors. Radom also has a special economic zone that offers incentives for new investors in the form of tax relief. The value of the relief is correlated with the number of new jobs created. The quality of the new jobs is generally not taken into account. During the panel discussions, some participants noted that one of the arguments used by the city to attract new investors is the low level of wages. On the other hand, the panellists emphasised that the quality of the jobs is becoming increasingly more important to new employees, especially youth deciding on their future career prospects. This clearly shows that more attention should be paid to the quality of the new jobs being created.

Local development projects and public procurement promote quality jobs

Local authorities also have other means of impacting the local labour markets, including through their own direct employment practices (in schools, hospitals, community services) as well as indirectly through purchasing products and services on the market. The recent crisis and growing fiscal deficit have forced public authorities to freeze wages in many segments of the public sector. This has caused a decrease in the real purchasing power of wages in the sector. There is also a trend to outsource some public sector services to private companies, which in some cases is linked with the decreasing quality of jobs (more flexible contracts, with lower employment protections and lower wages). This is particularly true of low-skilled jobs.

On the other hand, there is a growing interest in socially responsible public procurement. Some public authorities use a mechanism in the Polish public procurement law that allows the inclusion of social and employment aspects (social clauses) as assessment criteria in public procurement. However, their number is rather small and limited to those local authorities with a greater awareness. For example, in the Radomski sub-region, local actors are generally not aware of this approach and the opportunities it creates.

Another more popular approach is to apply an in-house scheme. Some local governments established social co-operatives that employ persons from disadvantaged groups. These co-operatives provide services to public institutions (such as cleaning, and gardening). One example is the "Poznańianka" social co-operative, described in the box below.

Box 3.9. **Poznańianka social co-operative as an example of promoting social value through public funds**

Poznańianka social co-operative was established in Poznań in 2013. This is an example of social established by local and regional authorities. The main objective of the co-operative is to provide work opportunities to indebted housing dwellers. The main activities are: cleaning, maintenance of green areas and reconstruction and construction works. Main clients of the co-operative come from the public sector: housing co-operatives, operator of municipal public transport, regional centre for social policy etc. There are currently over a dozen employees in the co-operative. Due to the fact that the co-operative was established by public agencies, local institutions are allowed to commission services to the co-operative without public procurement.

Source: http://poznanianka.spoldzielnie.org/.

Theme 4: Being inclusive

Figure 3.16. **Dashboard results: Being inclusive**

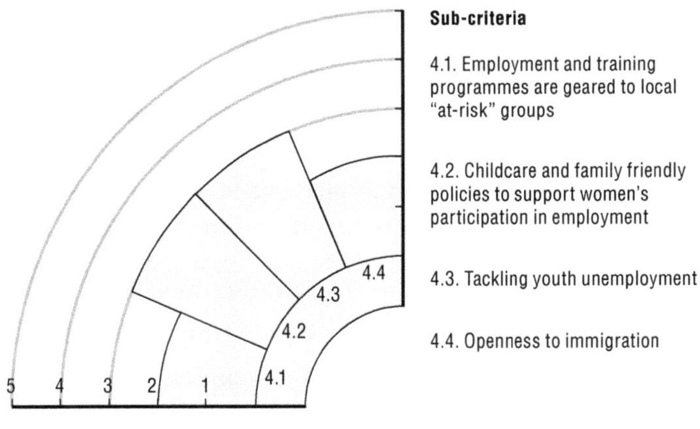

Employment and training programmes are geared to local "at-risk" groups

It is important to take into account the inclusiveness of local labour markets, particularly the opportunities provided to those with the most difficulty in securing a stable, decent job. These opportunities can be maximised through effective employment, education and integration services, targeted to "at-risk" groups, as well as by the creation of jobs for these groups.

According to the law, active labour market policy is geared to local "at-risk" groups. The Act on the promotion of employment indicates several groups in "particularly difficult situations on the labour market", i.e., youth (below 30 years of age), older persons (above 50 years of age), long-term unemployed persons, parents of children below 6 years of age, disabled persons, low skilled persons and women. Around 90% of the unemployed belong to at least one of these groups. In the case of Poznań, this percentage may be even higher due to the low level of unemployment.

Another measure of targeting is the OECD survey of poviat labour offices. As shown in the table below, almost all surveyed poviat labour offices report having programmes to meet the needs of youth, long-term unemployed, older workers, and people with disabilities, and most also have programmes for women and displaced workers as well.

Table 3.3. **Percentage of poviat labour offices that reported specific employment programmes are delivered that meet the needs of local disadvantaged groups, 2015**

	Percent of respondents
Youth	98.1
Long-term unemployed	97.6
Older workers	96.6
People with disabilities	96.2
Women	84.6
Displaced Workers	57.7
Ethnic minorities	7.7
Immigrants	6.7

Source: 2015 OECD LEED survey to poviat labour offices.

In practice, even among those who are in a "particularly difficult situation", the relatively better off are often the recipients of the services provided by poviat labour offices. Evidence of "creaming" can be seen by comparing the profiles of unemployed persons participating in training programmes financed by the employment office and the structure of all registered unemployed persons according to age and level of education. For example, in Poznań, there is an over-representation of middle-aged persons (25-34) and those with tertiary education, while older persons and those with a lower level of education, whose situation on the labour market is more difficult, were under-represented (PLOP, 2015).

This phenomenon is well documented and described in projects financed by ESF, where all project providers are obliged to achieve some level of effectiveness (PAG Uniconsult, 2015). Therefore, it can be assumed that the pressure to support those persons in a relatively better situation may even be strengthened by the new mechanisms of performance measurement and pay for success (described in chapter 2).

The recent reform of the labour offices reflected the acknowledgement that persons in the most difficult situations require special attention and more comprehensive services, which are sometimes beyond the capacity of poviat labour offices. To address this, the new profiling mechanisms assesses jobseekers into "profile III", with the idea that they should receive support services from local social assistance centres or non-governmental organisations. In August 2015, 31% of all registered unemployed were ascribed to profile III. Unfortunately, as described earlier, these persons often do not receive any support in practice due to the lack of resources in the social assistance centres (in the cases where

Figure 3.17. **Comparison of the structure of unemployed persons participating in training programmes and all registered unemployed according to level of education in Poznań and Poznański County, 2014**

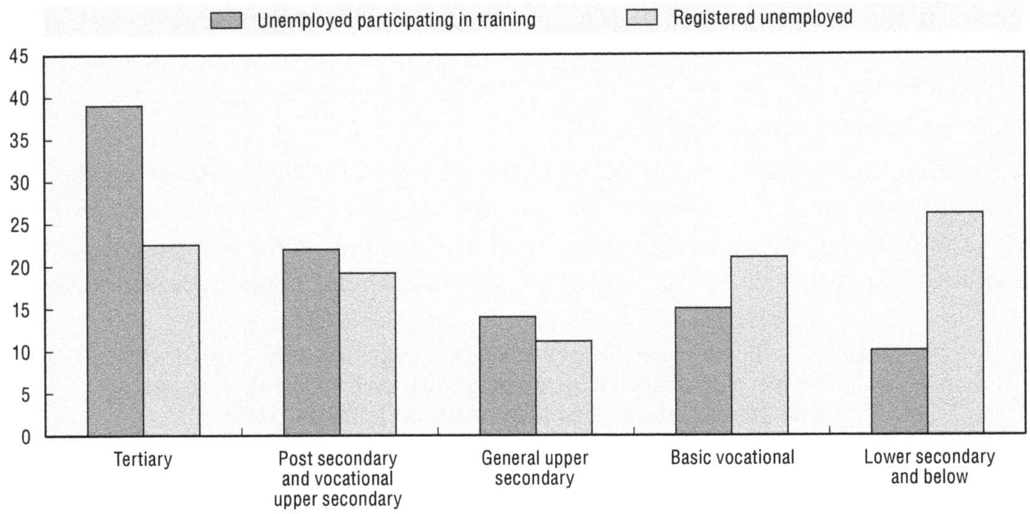

Source: PLOP (2015), *Rynek pracy Poznania i powiatu poznańskiego w 2014 roku [The labour market of Poznań and Poznański County in 2014)*, Poviat Labour Office in Poznań, Poznań.

Figure 3.18. **Comparison of the structure of unemployed persons participating in training programmes and all registered unemployed according to age in Poznań and Poznański County, 2014**

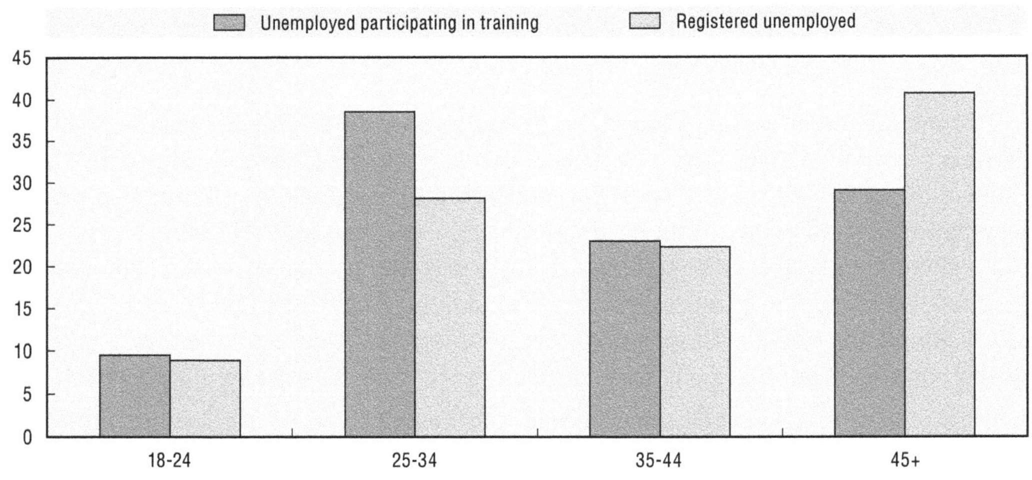

Source: PLOP (2015), *Rynek pracy Poznania i powiatu poznańskiego w 2014 roku [The labour market of Poznań and Poznański County in 2014)*, Poviat Labour Office in Poznań, Poznań.

they are not entitled to the services provided by the poviat labour office and are not covered by the services of the local social assistance centre).

Supportive, or wrap-around services, can also be critical. Access to services provided by poviat labour offices may be limited due to the cost of transportation, the lack of public transport as well as the unavailability of child care services. In such cases, the poviat labour office is able to finance child care while a client is attending training programmes or participating in other labour market instruments. The poviat labour office may also finance cost of transportation. Unemployed persons are also eligible for free public transportation on the days when they are using the services of poviat labour offices.

Unemployed persons in the most difficult situations who are not entitled to unemployment benefits,[5] can register at a local social assistance centre, which may also provide activation programmes and training opportunities for those at-risk. These activities are financed mostly by the ESF. The scale of the support is significant. In 2014, almost 70 000 clients of assistance centres participated in such projects, which is about 14% of all social assistance clients of working-age (MID, 2015). However, this is a case where "creaming" is often observed. A recent evaluation noted that the projects more often recruited persons who were relatively easier to activate and more promising in terms of potential professional activation, which directly contributed to the higher percentage of people taking up employment when the activities were completed (PAG Uniconsult, 2015).

Job creation and job placement are two popular instruments supporting disadvantaged persons. Job creation can take the form of supporting start-ups, as described in the previous subchapter. It is worth mentioning here that in 2014-2020, ESF resources for supporting entrepreneurship will be mostly targeted to persons in the most difficult employment situations: persons who are younger, older, long term unemployed, disabled, low-skilled and women.

Poviat labour offices also co-operate with employers, providing financial support for the creation of new jobs for the unemployed. The National Fund for the Rehabilitation of Disabled Persons can also support the creation of the new jobs. In 2014, about 1 000 such jobs were created.

Another important instrument is support for the social economy and the development of social enterprises, financed mostly by the ESF. The number of new social co-operatives has increased significantly during recent years, and 57% of them were created with support from the European Social Fund.

Figure 3.19. **Number of registered social co-operatives, Poland, 2002-14**

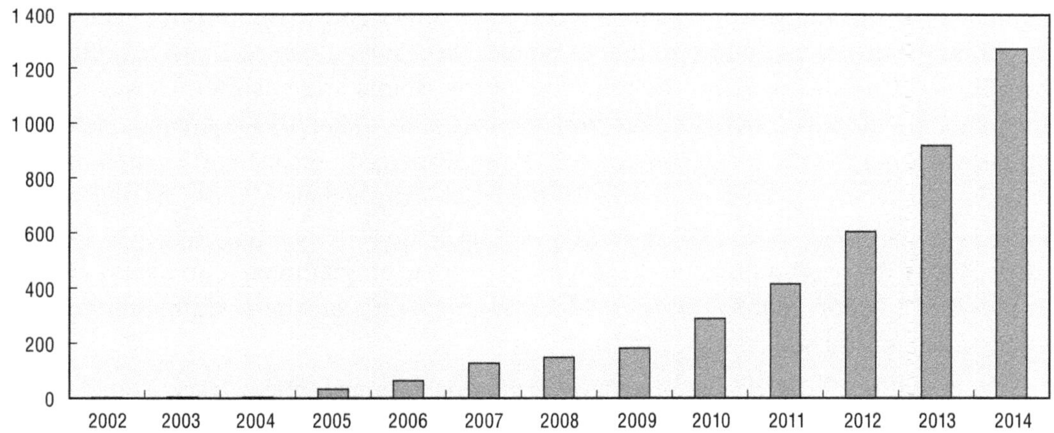

Source: National Auditing Association of Social Co-operatives (Ogólnoposki Związek Rewizyjny Spółdzielni Socjalnych); *http://ozrss.pl/spoldzielnie-socjalne/katalog/*.

The main purpose of establishing social co-operatives is to create jobs for persons with difficulties in securing employment, as well as to provide services to the local community. Even though some of the co-operatives established have not survived, and others are facing a rather difficult financial situation, there are numerous examples of successful co-operatives that provide jobs to persons in "at-risk" groups, such as the disabled, repeat offenders, youth, victims of violence, and Roma minority. The Wielkopolska Region is particularly active in this area, with the highest number of registered social co-operatives in the country (159).

Another instrument that supports job creation for disadvantaged groups is Vocational Activity Enterprises, where severely disabled persons can work and acquire professional experience. In 2014, there were 87 such enterprises, employing 3 500 disabled persons. About 70% of the costs of their employment is subsidised by the National Fund for the Rehabilitation of Disabled Person. Thus, the number of these enterprises and jobs for the disabled is relatively small and only a small number of disabled persons entitled to such services are employed through this instrument. Additionally, some experts emphasis the lack of incentives to enter the open labour market; therefore, most of the disabled working in such enterprises have been employed there for many years and the chances of others to work there are quite small.

In Poland, a number of instruments also exist outside of social enterprises or Vocational Activity Enterprises for the most vulnerable job-seekers. The basic instrument used by poviat labour offices, in close co-operation with local social assistance centres, is jobs in exchange for public benefits. In 2014, over 40 000 unemployed persons were employed in this type of work. Usually, these are persons in the most difficult situations, with the lowest skills and the worst prospects for becoming employed. Jobs for public benefits offers employment for 40 hours a month, with the minimum financial reward. The jobs are mostly organised by public institutions. However, in most cases, this instrument is not sufficient to lead to the regular employment of those involved. In practice, it is often used as a source of additional, temporary income by persons in the most difficult situations (PVLO, 2012).

The centres of social integration (CSI) offer a more comprehensive approach. Such centres can be operated either by NGOs or local governments. The centres provide social and employment integration programmes, namely assessment and support from a social worker, psychologist, and/or job advisor and a subsequent job placement. Training on the job can be organised both in the workshops of the centre or directly in the enterprise. The whole programme can last 12 or 18 months. In many cases, such a comprehensive, long-term programme is needed to solve the problems of the clients and ensure their sustainable integration on the labour market. However, the scale of these services is still insufficient. In 2013, there were 127 CSI in Poland and 6 900 disadvantaged persons participated in their activities. There were 24 such centres in Wielkopolska – the highest number in Poland – and there are at least three such centres in Poznań. The centres are relatively effective. In 2013, about 39% of those who finished participation in their programmes found some type of employment. Unfortunately, there is a lack of knowledge on the sustainability of this employment and its quality (CSO, 2014).

Co-operation at the local level to develop area-based approaches to tackle problems of spatially concentrated areas of disadvantage is still a challenge in Poland. Although there are many examples of good, effective local co-operation, it is still rather weak in many localities. A new impetus to better and more effective co-operation may be a new approach to revitalising disadvantaged urban and rural areas. Previous revitalisation programmes in Poland have had a rather limited impact on the situation of "at-risk" groups. New programmes financed by European funds will be oriented towards deprived areas and "at-risk" groups and should assume a comprehensive approach that combines infrastructure investment, employment and integration measures addressed to the local community. An example is the Integrated Programme of Renovation and Development of the City Centre of

Poznań 2014-20 which was prepared by the local authorities in Poznań. The programme addresses four areas: quality of living, economic, social and civic activity, culture, sustainable transportation and urban infrastructure. The programme will be implemented by a broad partnership, including the poviat labour office, the local centre of social assistance, local NGOs and other actors.

Childcare and family friendly policies to support women's participation in employment

The Labour Force Survey shows that one of the main reasons of young women's employment inactivity in Poland is their responsibility for caring for both children and older family members. Therefore, improvements in the access to affordable childcare services was identified as a key issue to address in the OECD's 2014 Economic Survey of Poland and is one of the main priorities of the Polish government. Local authorities are more aware of the importance of this service and are investing in new facilities. Consequently, access to childcare services has improved significantly during recent years. In 2003, only 36% of children at the age of 3-5 had access to childcare services and in 2014, this percentage had grown to 79%. It should be noted that this improvement has taken place particularly in sub-regions with poorer access to services. An example is the Radomski sub-region, where the participation rate in childcare has increased from 22% to 70%. It is still lower than the average for Poland, and there is still a 30% gap to attaining full coverage, but the difference between the Radomski sub-region and Poznań (where coverage is one of the highest in the country) has been substantially lowered. The improvement is financed mostly by local governments, but there have been some contributions from the European Social Fund and the state budget.

Figure 3.20. **Percentage of children aged 3-5 years old participating in childcare services, Radomski and Poznan sub-regions in comparison to Poland, 2003-14**

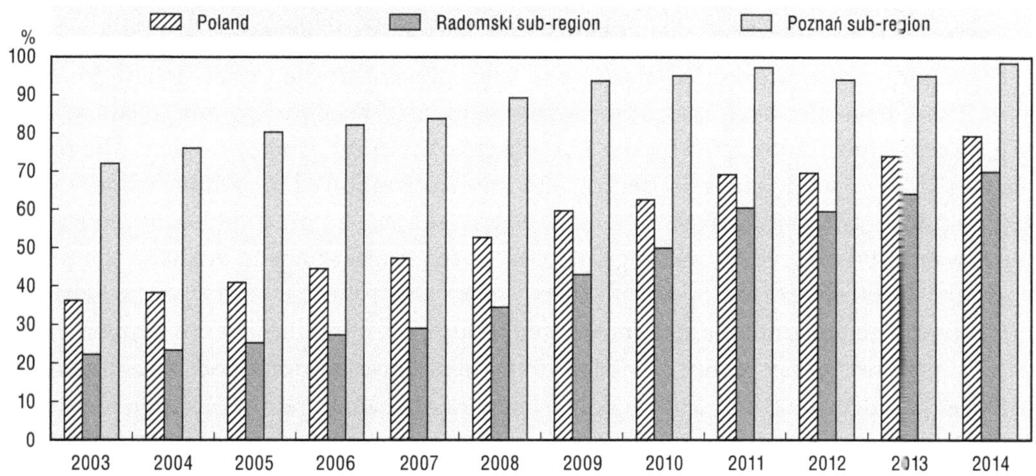

Source: Central Statistical Office, Local Data Bank.

As presented in the table below, access to childcare depends on the age of the child. There is a huge gap in access for children under the age of 3. On average only 5% of children at this age use childcare services, but this percentage is higher in large cities, including Poznań. Low access to childcare services for the youngest children still hampers the employment prospects of young parents, mostly women.

Table 3.4. **Percentage of children enrolled in childcare, by selected regions and sub-regions in Poland, 2013**

	Under the age of 3	Children aged 3-5
Poland	4.8	74.1
MAZOWIECKIE	5.4	80.2
Radomski sub-region	2.4	64.1
WIELKOPOLSKIE	4.0	77.6
City of Poznań	12.1	95.2

Source: Central Statistical Office, Local Data Bank.

The situation has been steadily improving. In 2011, a new law came into force on childcare for children up to three years of age and the "Toddler" programme. The new law introduced new, more flexible and less expensive forms of childcare (i.e., toddler's clubs and day nanny). The programme provides subsidies from the state budget for new and existing childcare slots. As a result, the number of childcare slots for children under the age of 3 has increased almost 2.5 times between 2011 and 2014, from 32 000 to 76 000 slots.

Besides access to childcare services, family friendly work organisation is another important issue that influences prospects for parents on the labour market. This type of work organisation still seems to be a privilege for a minority of employees, due to several reasons. In general, traditional forms of employment and the organisation of work-time are culturally preferred. The most common type of employment is the standard employment contact that features an eight-hour working day. Employees are resistant to more flexible forms of employment (part-time employment, temporary employment, employment on the basis of civil contracts, and self-employment) which in many cases are related to less attractive jobs, greater job instability, lower labour protections and unfavourable working hours (in the evenings or weekends). While employees are more in favour of the flexible organisation of work-time than flexible forms of employment, the majority still prefer stable, traditional work organisation and working hours (Sochańska-Kawiecka et al., 2013).

The issue of the work-life balance has been present in the public debate for many years. There have also been many projects implemented encouraging employers to adapt such policies, mostly financed by the European Social Fund. One example is the project "I have a child – I work; analysis, testing and implementation of innovative solutions that help reconcile work and private life in Wielkopolska, based on the idea of flexicurity", which was implemented by the Regional Centre for Social Policy in Poznań. The project promotes different forms of work-life balance, and finances childcare facilities in enterprises. The government also introduced a number of instruments to support family friendly policies in the labour law. However, these interventions and their impact on employer practices have not been solidly evaluated. It seems that these actions have only reached some employers, and mostly those who were already interested in such ideas.

Tackling youth unemployment

The recent financial crisis particularly impacted the situation of youth on the labour market. This is illustrated by the unemployment rate of persons aged 15-24 years, which increased from 12% in 2008 to 19% in 2013, and the increasing job insecurity of those already in employment. The group which is in a particularly difficult situation is young people who are neither in employment nor in education or training (NEET). According to

Figure 3.21. **Percentage of the young people neither in employment nor in education and training by age, Poland compared to European Union and OECD, 2014**

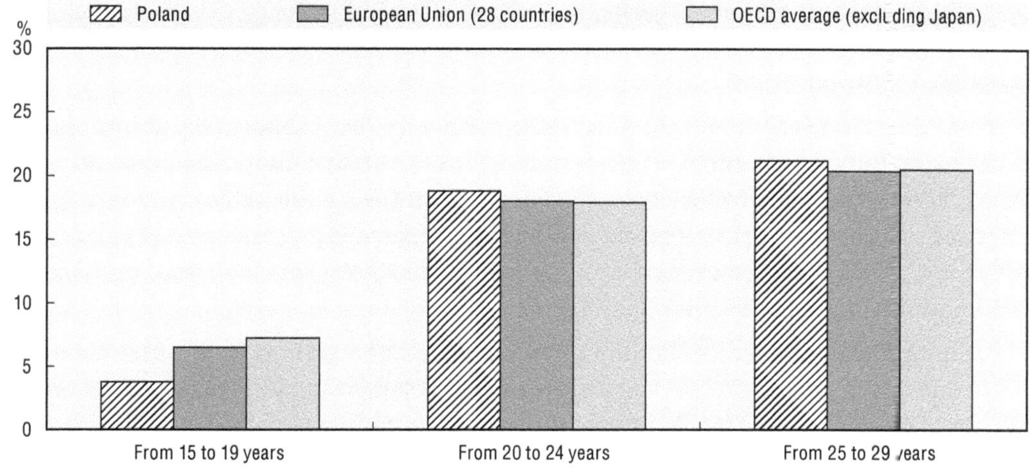

Source: OECD (2015), *Education at a Glance 2015: OECD Indicators*, OECD Publishing, Paris, *http://dx.doi.org/10.1787/eag-2015-en*.

Eurostat, in 2014, 15% of young people 15-29 years old were classified as NEET in Poland, which was close to EU average (15.4%). However, the probability of being in the NEET category increases with the age of the youth and is definitely higher amongst those who are 20 years of age or older.

The issue of youth employment has become one of the priorities of the Polish government. However, it should be noted that the situation of youth on the labour market is not a new challenge for Poland – as it presented difficulties through the transformation process. In fact, the youth unemployment rate reached 33% in 2002. Therefore, Poland has extensive experience in programmes addressed to this target group, which are mostly developed by the Ministry of Family, Labour and Social Policy.

In 2015, the Ministry of Family, Labour and Social Policy in co-operation with the Ministry of Economic Development (responsible for the European Social Fund in Poland), established a "Youth Guarantee" initiative targeted at NEETs. Activities will be mostly financed by the European Social Fund and implemented by poviat labour offices, NGOs, the Voluntary Labour Corps and institutions specialised in supporting youth. This partnership approach is strongly emphasised. The programme is addressed to four main groups, including:

- Young persons aged 15-17 years, who left education;
- Young persons aged 18-24 years, who are neither in employment nor in education and training, including persons requiring special support;
- Young persons aged 18-24 years, registered as unemployed, including students (part-time and evening students); and
- The graduates of schools and higher education institutions who remain unemployed 48 months after the completion of their education and unemployed 18-29 year- olds, supported in the area of entrepreneurship.

An individual action plan will be prepared for each person. During the first four months following registration at a poviat labour office, each young person should receive a job proposal, work experience, further education, or vocational training on-the-job or in a training facility. Graduates and unemployed persons aged between 18 and 29 can also receive entrepreneurship support in the form of a loan to establish a business. Besides this programme, other activities for youth will be implemented through poviat labour offices or the Voluntary Labour Corps (see earlier textbox).

Openness to immigration

Poland is a rather mono-ethnic country, with very low proportions of immigrants. According to the recent census of 2011, only 1.8% of the population was born outside of Poland. The percentage of those born outside of Poland is significantly higher among the oldest cohorts (70 years of age and older) and in regions which became part of Poland after the Second World War. The proportion of persons aged 20-49 years who were born outside of Poland is estimated to be 0.4% (CSO, 2013b).

Despite these numbers, Poland is seeing increasing migration from other countries. This is due to the growing relative attractiveness of Poland as a place to live. However, the strength of the pull factors which impact the scale of migration is much lower than in other EU or OECD countries. Local labour markets are also becoming more open to migrants and an increasing demand for labour is being observed in some branches. This can be illustrated by the result of a new, simplified procedure which enables employers to hire a foreigner for six months of a 12-month period on the basis of a declaration submitted to the poviat labour office. There were 410 000 such declarations submitted in the first half of 2015. About 98% of them were for citizens of Ukraine, with 60% of the declarations in agriculture and construction, two sectors where the employment of migrants is rather common. It should also be stressed that almost half of the declarations were submitted in the Mazowiecki Region. The new procedure is popular, mostly due to its simplicity and low cost. However, it is only available to citizens of selected countries.

Another area with a growing presence of migrants is higher education. Polish higher education institutions, which have enjoyed a boom of demand in the last two decades, now face a decreasing number of students, mostly due to demographic changes. Thus, some of them are actively trying to attract foreign students, as is particularly the case for higher education institutions in smaller cities. Studying in Poland is particularly popular among young Ukrainians, and in some faculties (e.g. medicine). One example is the Higher School of Economics in Radom, a private higher education institution, which attracted a group of 200 students from Ukraine. The school provides targeted services for migrant students, including language courses, assistance with settling and support in finding a job placement or employment.

Despite the positive examples described above, in general, support for migrants in Poland is rather limited and assessed by experts as inefficient (Grot et al., 2013). There is a small number of NGOs that specialise in supporting migrants and providing training and counselling; however, the scale of this type of support seems to be insufficient. There is a lack of specific programmes addressed to migrants that help them convert or upgrade their skills according to the needs of the local labour market. This also applies to language courses. Both in Poznań and Radom, some private language schools offer language training. This training is offered at different levels and can be adjusted to the needs of clients, but students must cover the full price of the course.

Migrants often need assistance to validate the competences that they attain informally or to recognise their diplomas and qualification. Immigrants to Poland often work in low-skill jobs, despite having advanced qualifications (OECD, 2015a). The basic mechanisms for recognising competences attained informally overseas is to pass external exams organised by Regional Examination Boards. This is the case for vocational qualifications. Also, some sectors have specific mechanisms, which enable the outcomes of prior learning to be recognised. However, there is a lack of data on the accessibility of these mechanisms to migrants. The recognition of qualification and skills from abroad is based on European legislation. The qualifications of regulated professions, such as physicians, can be recognised in Poland. Information on the process is provided by the Ministry of Science and Higher Education.

The main institution responsible for supporting migrants at the national level is the Ministry of Family, Labour and Social Policy. At the local level, county centres that support families are the main service providers and are social assistance system. However, the centres are usually unprepared for this task: their staff members are often untrained and the scope of services provided is rather limited. In Radom, the web site of the Municipal Assistance Centre has no information about support for migrants or contact details in languages other than Polish. The situation is the same in Poznań, although the probability of migrants looking for help in Poznań is much higher than in Radom.

Another key issue in Poland is the re-integration of returning Polish migrants returning to Poland after time abroad. However, this issue was outside of the scope of this analysis.

Notes

1. However, Radom serves as a very good example of an information system about VET offers at the local level for youth. It has an integrated management system of education, which presents the offer of all VET schools in Radom (description of occupations and qualifications), number of available placements and number of applications submitted. There are 18 VET schools presented in the system, with an average number of 4.2 occupations for each of them; however, the number of occupations is higher for VET at the ISCED 3c level than for those at the 3a level (5 and 3.4).
2. There is also a third category, informal education, which consists of learning activities undertaken outside of any formal or organisational structure (e.g. individual development).
3. There is very little information available about employers' opinions regarding the adequacy of training for adults. This topic requires further examination.
4. The OECD comparative figures only include start-up incentives take the form of continued payment of unemployment benefit during the start-up of a business, so do not capture spending on entrepreneurship training, for example. Therefore, they are not directly comparable to the Polish figures.
5. The unemployed are entitled to the unemployment benefit for six of twelve months after registration.

References

CEDEFOP (2015), *On the way to 2020: Data for vocational education and training policies. Country statistics overviews, www.cedefop.europa.eu/en/publications-and-resources/publications/5545.*

Coffey International Development (2012), *Ocena barier i luk prawnych w kontekście efektywnej realizacji wsparcia w ramach Europejskiego Funduszu Społecznego, (Evaluation of barriers and legal gaps for the effective realisation of the European Social Fund's support)*, Ministry of Regional Development, Warsaw.

CSO (2015), *Popyt na pracę, (Demand for labour)*, Central Statistical Office, Warsaw.

CSO (2014) *Centra integracji społecznej, zakłady aktywności zawodowej i warsztaty terapii zajęciowej w 2013 r.* [Social integration centres, enterprises of vocational activity and workshops for occupational therapy in 2013], Central Statistical Office, Warsaw.

CSO (2013a), *Kształcenie Dorosłych 2011 (Education of Adults 2011)*, Central Statistical Office, Warsaw.

CSO (2013b), *Ludność. Stan i struktura demograficzno-społeczna*, [Population, the status and demographic and social structure], Central Statistical Office, Warsaw.

Euridice (2012), *Entrepreneurship Education at School in Europe*; Education, Audiovisual and Culture Executive Agency, Brussels.

EurObser'ER (2013); *The stage of renewable energy in Europe*; Edition 2013, Paris.

Eurostat, *Labour market policy database*; *http://ec.europa.eu/eurostat/web/labour-market/labour-market-policy*.

Giguère,S. and F. Froy (eds.) (2009), *Flexible Policy for More and Better Jobs*, Local Economic and Employment Development (LEED), OECD Publishing, Paris, *http://dx.doi.org/10.1787/9789264059528-en*.

Grot, K. and J. Segeš-Frelak (2013), *W poszukiwaniu nowych wzorów integracji cudzoziemców*, [In the search of new patterns of integration of foreigners], Institute of Public Affairs, Warsaw.

Hattie, J. (2009), *Visible learning, A synthesis of over 800 meta-analyses relating to achievement*, Routledge, London and New York.

Herbst, M. (2012) *Zarządzanie Oświatą* [Management of education], ICM, Warsaw.

IBC (2014), *Przeprowadzenie monitoringu i ewaluacji projektu pilotażowego pn. "Partnerstwo dla Pracy* [Monitoring and evaluation of the pilot project "Partnership for the job"], IBC Group, Warsaw.

IER (2013), *Umiejętności Polaków – wyniki Międzynarodowego Badania Kompetencji Osób Dorosłych (PIAAC)*, [Skills of Poles – the results of the Programme of International Assessment of Adults Competences (PIAAC)], Institute of Educational Research, Warsaw.

IER (2014), *Polish teachers and principals – an international perspective, Key findings of TALIS 2013*, Institute of Educational Research, Warsaw.

Kocór, M., A. Strzebońska and M. Dawid-Sawicka (2015), *Rynek pracy widziany oczami pracodawców. Na podstawie badań pracodawców i ofert pracy zrealizowanych w 2014 roku w ramach V edycji projektu Bilans Kapitału Ludzkiego*, [The labour market in the eyes of employers. On the basis of research of employers and job completed in 2014 within the V edition of the Balans of Human Capital], Polish Agency for Enterprise Development, Warsaw, *http://bkl.parp.gov.pl*.

Kołodziejska, A. (2012), *Można, czy nie można nauczyć przedsiębiorczości w szkole?, [Is it possible to learn enterpreneurship in school?]*, rynekpracy.org, *http://rynekpracy.org/wiadomosc/764239.html*.

MID (2015), *Sprawozdanie roczne z realizacji PO KL w roku 2014, [Annual report on HC OP implementation in 2014]*, Ministry of Infrastructure and Development Warsaw, *www.efs.2007-2013.gov.pl*.

MLMO (2015), *Zapotrzebowanie na kwalifikacje i kompetencje zawodowe na mazowieckim rynku pracy*, [The demand for professional qualifications and competence for the labour market of Mazowieckie voivodship], Mazovian Labour Market Observatory, Warsaw, *http://obserwatorium.mazowsze.pl/badania-i-analizy/badanie-pracodawcow*.

MLMO (2013), *Rola doradztwa zawodowego, [The role of vocational guidance]*, Mazovian Labour Market Observatory, Warsaw.

MLMO (2012), *Współpraca pracodawców i organizacji pracodawców ze szkołami zawodowymi – badanie jakościowe w subregionach [Co-operation of employers and employers organisations with vocational schools – qualitative research in sub-regions]*; Mazovian Labour Market Observatory, Warsaw, *http://obserwatorium.mazowsze.pl/pliki/files/raport_wspolpraca_final.pdf*.

MLMO (2011a), *Badania efektywności kształcenia ustawicznego i zapotrzebowania na kształcenie ustawiczne. Raport cząstkowy dla powiatu radomskiego oraz powiatów dodatkowych z subregionu radomskiego, [The research on the effectiveness of continuing education and demand for the lifelong learning. Interim report for the poviat of Radom and other poviats within radomski sub-region.]*, Mazovian Labour Market Observatory, Warsaw, *http://obserwatorium.mazowsze.pl/badania-i-analizy/ksztalcenie-ustawiczne*.

MLMO (2011b), *Formy nauki zawodu* [Forms of vocational education], Mazovian Labour Market Observatory, Warsaw.

MLSP (2015a), *Szczegółowe informacje o wydatkach Funduszu Pracy w latach 2006-2014 i plan 2015*, [Detailed information on Labour Fund spending between 2006-2014 and plans for 2015], Ministry of Labour and Social Policy, Warsaw.

MLSP (2015b) *Informacja o stanie i strukturze zatrudnienia w wojewódzkich i powiatowych urzędach pracy w 2014 roku*, [Information on stock and structure of employment in regional and local labour offices in 2014], Ministry of Labour and Social Policy, Warsaw.

MLSP (2015c), *Statystyki strukturalne sierpień 2015*, [Structural statistics August 2015], Ministry of Labour and Social Policy, Warsaw, August, *http://psz.praca.gov.pl/rynek-pracy/statystyki-i-analizy/bezrobocie-rejestrowane*.

MLSP (2015d), *Efektywność podstawowych form aktywizacji zawodowej realizowanych w ramach programów na rzecz promocji zatrudnienia i łagodzenia skutków bezrobocia i aktywizacji zawodowej w 2014 r.* [Efficiency of the basic forms of vocational activisation realised in the frame of the active labour market policy in 2014], Ministry of Labour and Social Policy, Warsaw.

MLSP (2014a), *Profilowanie pomocy dla osób bezrobotnych; Podręcznik dla pracowników powiatowych urzędów pracy* [Profiling support for the unemployed; Manual for employees of poviat labour offices], Ministry of Labour and Social Policy, Warsaw.

MLSP (2014b), *Szkolenia, staże i inne formy wspierania podnoszenia kwalifikacji bezrobotnych*, [Training and apprenticeships and other forms of developing the qualifications of the unemployed], Ministry of Labour and Social Policy, Warsaw.

MLSP (2009) *Analiza działalności rad zatrudnienia i ich wpływ na kształtowanie polityki rynku pracy w okresie 2004-2008;* [The analysis of employment councils and their influence on policy the labour market in the period 2004-2008], Ministry of Labour and Social Policy, Warsaw.

MLSP (2008), *Analiza funkcjonowania urzędów pracy po ich włączeniu do administracji samorządowej* [Analysis of the functioning of labour offices after their incorporation to local government], Ministry of Labour and Social Policy, Warsaw.

MRD (2012), *Ewaluacja komplementarności i efektywności wsparcia instytucji otoczenia biznesu świadczących usługi dla przedsiębiorców [Evaluation of complementarity and effectiveness of support of institutions supporting business]*; Warsaw.

NCSVCE (2013), *Stan szkolnictwa zawodowego w Polsce – raport, [The state of vocational education in Poland – report]*, National Centre of Supporting Vocational and Continuous Education, Warsaw.

National Auditing Association of Social Co-operatives (Ogólnoposki Związek Rewizyjny Spółdzielni Socjalnych), *http://ozrss.pl/spoldzielnie-socjalne/katalog/*.

NCSVET (2015), *Budowanie zaufania do kształcenia zawodowego. Monitorowanie procesu wdrażania podstaw programowych kształcenia w zawodach 2013-2015 [Building trust to vocational education. The monitoring of the implementation of core curricula of vocational education 2013-2015]*, National Centre of Supporting Vocational and Continuous Education, Warsaw, *www.koweziu.edu.pl*.

OECD (2016a), *OECD Economic Surveys: Poland 2016*, OECD Publishing, Paris, *http://dx.doi.org/10.1787/eco_surveys-pol-2016-en*.

OECD (2016b), "Labour market programmes: expenditure and participants", *OECD Employment and Labour Market Statistics* (database). DOI: *http://dx.doi.org/10.1787/data-00312-en* (accessed on 2 March 2016).

OECD (2016c), "Labour Market Statistics: Employment by permanency of the job", *OECD Employment and Labour Market Statistics* (database), *http://dx.doi.org/10.1787/data-00296-en* (accessed on 8 March 2016).

OECD (2014), *OECD Economic Surveys: Poland 2014*, OECD Publishing, Paris, *http://dx.doi.org/10.1787/eco_surveys-pol-2014-en*.

OECD (2011), *Zatrudnienie i rozwój lokalny w Polsce w kontekście zmian klimatycznych; [Employment and local development in Poland in the context of the climate change]*, Ministry of Regional Development, Warsaw.

PAG Uniconsult (2015), *Badanie skuteczności wsparcia realizowanego w ramach komponentu regionalnego PO KL 2007-2013* (The research on efficiency of support provided in the frame of the regional component of Human Capital Operational Program 2007-2013); Warsaw.

PAED (2014), *Bariery wzrostu; Panel polskich przedsiębiorców; materiały konferencyjne, [Barriers of the growth. Panel of the Polish enterprises. Conference materials]*, Polish Agency for Enterprise Development, Warsaw, *http://badania.parp.gov.pl/files/74/75/77/597/22739.pdf*.

PAED (2009), *Jak inwestować w rozwój pracowników o niskch kwalifikacjach*, [How to invest in the development of low-skilled workers], Polish Agency for Enterprise Development, Warsaw.

PLOP (2015), *Rynek pracy Poznania i powiatu poznańskiego w 2014 roku*, [Labour market of Poznan and poznanski poviat in 2014], Poviat Labour Office in Poznan, Poznan.

PVLO (2012), *Analiza programu prac społecznie użytecznych in the podlskie voivodship*, [Analyse of the programme of the social benefit works in the podlaskie voivodship], Podlaskie Voivodship Labour Office, Białystok.

ROLMW (2014), *Zapotrzebowanie wielkopolskiego rynku pracy na kwalifikacje i kompetencje zawodowe*, [Needs of the Regional Labour Market for Qualifications and Competences], Regional Observatory of the Labour Market for the Wielkopolska, Poznań, *www.obserwatorium.wup.poznan.pl/php/160.php*.

SAO (2015), *Skuteczność wybranych form aktywnego przeciwdziałania bezrobociu w niektórych województwach [The effectiveness of selected active forms of counteracting unemployment in some voivodeships]*, Supreme Audit Office, Warsaw.

Sochańska-Kawiecka, M., A. Morysińska, E. Makowska-Belta, Z. Kołakowska-Seroczyńska, R. Szarfenberg and T. Mering (2013), *Elastyczne formy zatrudnienia – skutki społeczne i ekonomiczne*; [Flexible forms of employment – social and economic effects], Laboratorium Badań Społecznych, Wrocław.

Sudak, I. (2015), *100 tys. miejsc pracy w ekologicznej energii*, [100 thousands job places in the ecological energy], Gazeta Wyborcza, 28.09.2015, *http://wyborcza.biz/biznes/1,147744,18923204,100-tys-miejsc-pracy-w-ekologicznej-energii.html*.

VLO (2015), *Raport roczny 2014*, [Annual Report 2014], Voivodship Labour Office, Warsaw.

Chapter 4

Towards an action plan for jobs in Poland: Recommendations and best practices

Stimulating job creation at the local level requires integrated actions across employment, training, and economic development portfolios. Co-ordinated place-based policies can help workers find suitable jobs, while also contributing to demand by stimulating productivity. This requires policies which can be catered to the local level, up-to-date and accurate data, and integrated partnerships which leverage the efforts of stakeholders. This chapter outlines the key recommendations emerging from the review of local job creation policies in Poland.

Overall recommendations

Better aligning programmes and policies to local economic development

- Carefully monitor the new PES reforms and adjust as necessary to prevent unintended consequences and to allow for tailoring to local conditions.
- Improve local co-ordination of employment and skills policies and programmes.
- Increase the availability and use of data at the sub-national level and build a stronger evaluation culture.

Adding value through skills

- Make the VET system more responsive to local labour market needs, including through better engagement of employers in designing and delivering VET.
- Expand offerings to improve basic skills.

Targeting policy to local employment sectors and investing in quality jobs

- Focus on improving skills utilisation and work organisation.
- Promote economic development that is inclusive and contributes to the creation of quality jobs, including through more strategic use of public procurement.
- Ensure that adequate guidance and information on career pathways are available to both youth and adults, and that it is informed by local labour market assessments.

Being inclusive

- Address gaps in services for most disadvantaged clients of the public employment service, particularly those classified into the third profile.
- Improve access to child care services, particularly for children aged 0-3 years of age.

Recommendations for use of ESF

- Pilot new approaches to local co-ordination through the development of local skills councils or strengthening local labour market councils.
- Expand on work already undertaken to use information from Social Insurance Institutions to evaluate ESF-financed projects to other labour market programmes.
- Strengthen the VET sector by (1) supporting the development of regional networks of vocational schools; (2) financing local intermediaries between employers and VET institutions; and/or (3) facilitate sharing of best practices across VET institutions.
- Support projects that fill the gap in basic skills offerings.
- Support projects that seek to improve work organisation and boost skills utilisation.
- Extend the range of ESF-funded instruments and services available to clients classified into Stream III.

Additional recommendations for case study areas

Poznań sub-region

- Build on the strong tradition of apprenticeship in crafts enterprises by expanding this model to other sectors and occupations.
- Focus on retaining highly skilled workers and students, by ensuring university education aligns with local labour market demands and working with employers to maximise the use of skills.
- Establish pilot programmes, which encourage employers to think more strategically about their workforce and human resources management to promote quality jobs.

Radomski sub-region

- Build the capacity of local employment services by increasing the number staff in the poviat labour offices.
- Focus on job quality, not just quantity in attracting inward investments and making job placements. Examine how best to introduce social clauses which encourage apprenticeship and other work-based training into procurement processes.
- Expand child care services for children age 3-5 to catch up to national coverage rates.

Better aligning programmes and policies to local economic development

Recommendation: Carefully monitor the new PES reforms and adjust as necessary to prevent unintended consequences

The 2014 reform of public employment services described in Chapter 2 represents important progress. Like many countries across the OECD, Poland has taken steps to strengthen its performance management systems, including creating stronger incentives for local PES offices to meet the key performance measures defined at the national level. At the same time, these reforms will need to be carefully monitored to identify and avert any unintended negative consequences. While this recommendation focuses specifically on the performance management system for PES offices themselves, many of the same issues are relevant for the payment-by-results contracts of contracted providers. Other issues related to the new mechanism of profiling are addressed in a separate recommendation.

In particular, two areas raise concerns. Given the increased emphasis and incentives put in place to meet performance management objectives, there is a risk of poviat labour offices "gaming" the system to inflate performance measures through methods such as "creaming" (only serving the most employable clients) or other types of "creative accounting". This system may also encourage PES offices to rapidly place clients into jobs, even if these jobs are a bad skills match or of low quality. While the latter may technically meet the performance indicator requirements, it can undermine the productive potential of local economies, as it promotes poor quality jobs and skills mismatches. Some of these challenges could be partially eliminated by more sophisticated methods of measuring the effects of active labour market policies, such as:

- Extending the period for which effectiveness is measured (to six months and 12 months);
- Delegating the task of measuring the effects of poviat labour offices to an independent body; or
- Measuring the net effects of active labour market policies on the basis of data from the IT systems of employment offices and social insurance data (an experimental measurement using these sources was already conducted by the Chancellery of the Prime Minister).

The other key concern is that the current performance management system allows for no adaptation or tailoring to local circumstances in terms of broader economic and labour market characteristics or specificities of the clients served. Across the OECD, many PESs measure local inputs and outputs as part of performance management, but few actually use detailed information on jobseeker characteristics and local labour markets as recommended by the OECD (OECD, 2015). Such practices can help to ensure that local labour offices are being measured using a fair yardstick, while reducing the incentives for creaming (in the case where performance measures are adjusted for types of clients served). Performance management systems in the United States, Australia, Germany and Switzerland have incorporated these practices. The German and Swiss models are described in more detail in the textbox below.

Box 4.1. **Performance management in other countries**

Germany: using benchmarking and negotiation to identify local targets. In Germany, setting performance targets is somewhat of an iterative process involving national, regional and local tier of governance, with social partners involved throughout. At the federal level, a Board of Governors with tripartite representation works with the government to jointly appoint a three person management board responsible for the operational management of the PES (Bundesagentur für Arbeit). This national tier develops broad targets and sometimes binding operational guidelines, which are handed down to the regional (Lander) tier of management. Local agencies, in turn, make proposals to the regional tiers about their expected level of performance. The regional directors then scrutinise and aggregate these targets, before sending a proposal back to the national tier. Consensus is reached through discussions between the national and regional tier. Evidence suggests that this negotiation process is fully used, with examples of regional and local requests for lower performance targets both being accepted and rejected at the regional and national level.

Box 4.1. **Performance Management in Other Countries** *(cont.)*

Additionally, the Institute of Employment Research of the Federal Employment Agency has used advanced statistical modelling to cluster local labour markets into 12 comparable groups to help benchmark and motivate performance. In discussions with PES, key labour market indicators were selected, and regression analysis was used to identify their key determinants. Cluster analysis was then used to sort groups that are similar in terms of the key determinants, allowing for comparisons of "likes and likes". Examples of these groups include rural areas with a good labour market situation and strong seasonal dynamics, areas with SME structure and good labour market situation, areas mainly characterised by big cities with moderately high unemployment, etc. (See Blien et al 2010 for more detail). The highest performing agencies in each cluster serve as a benchmark the others in that cluster try to reach.

Switzerland: using regressions to adjust performance measurement to local conditions. In 2000, Switzerland introduced a system for rating local performance in terms of off-benefit outcomes. Using a rich array of information on job-seeker characteristics from the PES administrative database as well as survey-based information about local labour markets, the Ministry uses regression-adjusted formulas to publish comparative ratings of local office performance. There are four regularly monitored primary indicators of PES performance which are assigned different weights:

- Speed of reintegration of the unemployed into the labour market, as measured by the average duration of unemployment benefit entitlement per unemployed (weighted 50%).
- Prevention of long-term unemployment, as measured by the share of those remaining unemployed among those who were registered as unemployment benefit recipients 13 months before (weighted 20%).
- Prevention of benefit exhaustion, as measured by the share of unemployed no longer entitled to federal unemployment benefits in the total number of unemployed (weighted 20%).
- Prevention of repeated registration for benefit, as measured by the share of previous unemployed who have de-registered but re-apply for unemployment benefits within four months (weighted 10%).

While initially, this rating was intended to be feed into federal PES funding formulas to the cantons, this link was terminated after criticism from the cantons. Instead, the system functions by providing offices performance data in order to better manage their own offices; through "naming and shaming" and peer pressure; and the possibility of an in-depth evaluation undertaken by the ministry should offices repeatedly underperform. However, this system is not without its challenges. Using exits from UI, rather than proven entry to a job, as the outcome measure means that outcomes for people without a UI entitlement are not taken into account. Therefore, all else being equal, focusing on reducing the number of UI recipients will result in a higher rating than priortising social assistance beneficiaries.

Source: OECD (2015), *OECD Employment Outlook 2015*; Blien, U., F. Hirschenauer and P. thi Hong Van (2010), "Classification of Regional Labour Markets for Purposes of Labour Market Policy", *Papers in Regional Science*, Vol. 9, No. 4, November. European Commission (2013), *Review of Performance Management in Public Employment Services*, Brussels, Author: Alex Nunn. European Commission (2012), *Performance management in Public Employment Services*, Brussels, Author: Alex Nunn.

Recommendation: Improve local co-ordination of employment and skills policies and programmes

At the local level, a number of actors work on skills and labour market policy, including poviat labour offices, NGOs, private training institutions, VET, local social assistance institutions, universities, and there is a need to strengthen co-operation between all these actors. Past OECD research has highlighted the important role that strong local governance boards can play in bringing together key stakeholders in steering the provision of skills and/or employment policy locally. The existence of local labour market councils, which bring together representatives of employer's organisations, trade unions, and NGOs, are already a step in this direction. However, a combination of low capacity and relatively little statutory authority beyond an advisory role limits the strategic role they play in practice. Concerns were also raised about potential conflicts of interest for labour market councils in smaller poviats.

Combining and coordinating the efforts of all actors acting at the local level could take the form of a local partnership, local platform for skills or local skills councils. In the case of larger local labour markets (such as Radom or Poznań), this could also include some sectoral councils. Such structures could serve as a mechanism to develop local sectoral strategies and ensure that the investments in skills are adjusted to local needs. In the past, there have been some initiatives targeted toward building local partnerships. However, a significant number of them have not succeeded. In order to avoid the risk of creating artificial partnerships, it is better to adopt a step by step approach – building smaller partnerships at the beginning, focused on some sectors, but paired with some authority to make real decisions regarding programmes and funding. ESF resources could be used to implement a pilot project, testing the proposed approach of local partnerships in several communities. The ESF could support this work, for example by funding projects addressed to labour market, training, vocational education and social integration coordinated by these bodies.

Another approach would be to focus on strengthening labour market councils rather than setting up new institutional arrangements or structures. In practice, this would require stepwise increases in capacity and authority, as improvements in one will not be beneficial without improvements in the other. This could be done in several ways, such as through a national capacity building or technical assistance programme for all labour market councils linked to specific statutory authority, seconding staff to help support the functioning of the boards, or providing incremental authority for labour market councils, starting with those that have demonstrated the strongest capacities to date. ESF may be particularly beneficial, for example, in supporting capacity building programmes or seconded staff. The box below provides two examples of programmes to improve local capacities in other OECD countries.

Box 4.2. **Approaches to Building Local Level Capacities**

Community Capacity Building in Newfoundland and Labrador. The Department of Innovation, Business and Rural development in Newfoundland and Labrador Canada offers a community capacity building programme to economic development organisations in order to build their capacity to be partners in regional economic development. The programme provides non-repayable contributions to not-for-profit economic development organisations such as municipalities, industry/sector groups, educational institutions and any other community

Box 4.2. **Approaches to Building Local Level Capacities** *(cont.)*

based organisation involved in economic development. In addition, it provides training and supports development sessions based on a series of certified programme modules. These modules include sessions on the following topics: strategic planning, relationship building, organisational skills and management and co-operative development.

Strong Cities, Strong Communities. In order to help the American cities hardest hit by the recession, the Strong Cities, Strong Communities (SC2) initiative is a new model of federal-local collaboration, intended to improve how the federal government works with local governments to further job creation and local economic development. It includes several strands. Interagency federal SC2 teams work with selected cities to help them better navigate existing federal agencies and programmes while providing technical assistance and expertise. Additionally, through the SC2 fellowship programme, early- to mid-career professionals complete 2 year fellowships in mayor's offices or local government agencies to assist in the design and implementation of strategic projects. Another strand is the economic visioning challenge, through which federal supports are provided to cities to help them implement a "challenge competition" in which teams of professionals submit economic development proposals, with the best proposal receiving a financial prize. Finally, through the SC2 National Resource Network, several types of technical assistance are available, including direct support, access to peer networks, and on-line tools and resources.

Source: Skinner, G. (2012), "Department of Innovation, Business and Rural Development, Government of Newfoundland and Labrador", *OECD Conference*, October 2012, *www.oecd.org/rural/krasnoyarsk/3%20Gillian%20Skinner_MR2_Skill%20Building_ENG.pdf*; White House Council (2013), "Strong Cities, Strong Communities Initiative", *1st Annual Report*, April 2013, *www.huduser.org/portal/publications/pdf/huddoc.pdf*.

Recommendation: Increase the availability and use of data at the sub-national level and build a stronger evaluation culture.

In order to design and implement appropriate, well targeted employment and skills programmes, there is a need for in-depth knowledge about current and future labour market needs and skills gaps. The analyses should be conducted at least at the sub-regional level and take into account sectoral specifics. Otherwise, there is a risk of generating findings that are too general and of low utility. It is also critically important to make sure that the analyses will be presented in a user-friendly form. The academic approach of presenting findings, which is unfortunately often present in reports, should be avoided.

This task could be conducted by regional observatories of the labour market, which exist in almost each region, as well as regional territorial observatories. Of critical importance is developing a sound methodology for assessing labour market needs as well as for forecasting future needs and trends at the sub-regional level. The methodology could be developed in close co-operation with the Ministry of Family, Labour and Social Policy, Ministry of Economic Development (which coordinates the network of regional territorial observatories) as well as representatives of regions, social partners and experts. One example of an approach taken in the United States is described in Box 4.3.

In order to facilitate the ongoing improvement of programme quality and efficiency, poviat labour offices, VET institutions and other actors should regularly receive information about the situation of their clients after they have completed a programme, training or vocational education. Currently, poviat labour offices analyse only short-term information (3 months after programme completion), which is insufficient to make sound

Box 4.3. The Workforce Intelligence Network, Michigan, US

The Workforce Intelligence Network (WIN) provides opportunities for co-ordination and innovation across partners by delivering actionable marketplace intelligence to support more efficient solutions for employers. This information helps consortium members, particularly community colleges, make better "real time" decisions regarding skill gaps. One of the tools used by WIN is a methodology to search the internet for job openings and resumés. This information, combined with data from the state's labour market information and special surveys, is incorporated in strategic plans and operational decisions. For example, SEMCA (the local Workforce Investment Board that manages employment services) has been able to act upon this information and is currently working to create a talent pool for Computerised Numerical Control and Welding. SEMCA also relies on WIN for detailed analysis of specific industries and occupations. Each year it completes a "Region Top Jobs" report, which includes the availability of current and projected opportunities by occupation, with the number of openings, and the rates of pay.

Within the advanced manufacturing sector, WIN connects with various organisations and associations and is leading important initiatives to better align the talent system with talent needs. WIN serves as project lead and fiscal agent for InnoState – a new coalition among WIN, the Detroit Regional Chamber's Connection Point, the Michigan Manufacturing Technology Centre, the National Centre for Manufacturing Sciences, the Business Accelerators of Southeast Michigan, and the Society of Manufacturing Engineers. Backed by funding from the Michigan Economic Development Corporation and various federal government agencies, InnoState is focused on expanding the New Product Contract Manufacturing Cluster of firms to increase their business and compete globally. WIN also convenes the skilled trades taskforce, which addresses employer talent needs through ongoing dialogue between the talent system and employers looking for skilled trades talent.

In the area of IT, which includes some of the fastest growing firms in the region, WIN's cluster strategy includes the convening of an employer-led, multi-industry council, which has come to be known as the Tech Council of Southeast Michigan. The Council is convened to raise awareness of and shape community responses to regional talent needs. This group meets routinely and has two primary foci: talent attraction and development; and marketing and branding Southeast Michigan as a technology hub.

The Council is comprised of more than 30 employers who have a significant need for information technology talent and is open to any additional company who may be interested in participating. WIN is directly involved with company-led training initiatives like 'IT in the D' and serves as a communication conduit for the region's various talent partners. WIN is also working closely with the Michigan Economic Development Corporation, the State of Michigan, business accelerators, and many others to collaborate and help drive their efforts and programmes aimed at closing the IT talent gap in Southeast Michigan.

Source: OECD (2014a), "Employment and Skills Strategies in the United States", *OECD Reviews on Local Job Creation*, OECD Publishing, Paris, *http://dx.doi.org/10.1787/9789264209398-en*.

and reliable conclusions about programme effectiveness. Thus, the approach should be redefined, with a stronger focus on long-term employment effects, including the stability of the job as well as the quality of employment.

In order to improve the reliability of the above-mentioned monitoring and data, it is recommended that co-operation be strengthened with Social Insurance Institutions (ZUS), which can provide accurate and up-to-date information on participants' actual situation on the labour market. In fact, poviat labour offices already co-operate with ZUS, and the Ministry of Economic Development is already working with ZUS on developing a monitoring system of the results of ESF-financed programmes. This demonstrates that such co-operation and exchange of information is possible, with ZUS providing long-term information on the status of participants on the labour market, the stability of employment as well as the level of wages.

It is also important to develop the culture and practice of evaluating local employment, training and VET programmes. Evaluation should provide information on actual effects, taking into consideration side effects (e.g. deadweight), as well as a better understanding of the actual needs of recipients, what works, why and how to improve the programmes. Taking into consideration that there may be not enough skills and capacity at the local level to conduct a good quality evaluation, this task could be managed at the regional level.

Adding value through skills

Recommendation: Make the VET system more responsive to local labour market needs, including through better engagement of local employers

A clear gap identified through this work was a misalignment between the VET system and local labour market needs. During the local roundtables, stakeholders estimated that employers found 70% of the curriculum in VET programmes irrelevant. Rather than being responsive to local labour market needs, VET programme offerings appear to be much more "path dependent" in that they are determined by the capacity and previous experience of existing VET institutions, including the profile and competences of VET teachers and equipment. While some promising examples do exist – such as the Centre for Practical Education in Radom and the vocational school in Centre for Practical Education in Radomędz – overall more could be done in this area.

One important step would be better engaging employers in VET systems, both in the day-to-day practicalities of offering work-based learning opportunities as well as at a more strategic level in determining local VET provision and curriculum. Well-prepared staff could mediate between schools and employers, helping schools to better understand the needs of employers and accordingly adjust the curriculum and practice of vocational education. These agents could be employed by local authorities and trained by the National Centre for Supporting Vocational and Continuing Education. Another approach would be setting-up advisory councils, as demonstrated in Box 4.4. Regardless of the approach taken, what is critical is having some type of mechanism for better linking these two groups of stakeholders.

Strong and engaged employer associations can also play a critical role in supporting and improving VET provision. For example, in Wielkopolska, there is a strong tradition of apprenticeship in crafts enterprises, with the local craft association playing a key role. While not all local areas have this type of strong local employer associations, important progress is already being made with the Polish Agency for the Development of Entrepreneurship setting up sector councils. Going forward, attention will need to be paid to how these national developments can translate to strong associations at the local level as well.

The experience of the staff of VET schools which have successfully co-operated with local employers in establishing high quality vocational education should be regarded as a resource that could be used to improve other VET institutions. This resource could be leveraged through a coaching programme, which engages professionals from successful

Box 4.4. Programme Advisory Committees in Ontario, Canada's Community Colleges

In Ontario, Canada, Program Advisory Committees composed of employers help to ensure that community colleges are educating and training graduates with the right skills for current job markets. They are a critical resource in ensuring the relevancy and application of college programs and meeting the needs of business and industry, and also provide community colleges with an early "heads up" to capitalise on emerging trends and new technologies. These committees, reporting through the president, are responsible to the Board of Governors, and play an instrumental role in the development of new programs and the monitoring of existing programs. Some of the primary responsibilities of Programme Advisory Committee are to:

- Advise college staff in defining graduate profiles and program learning outcomes;
- Provide input into the development and evaluation of the curriculum;
- Recommend and assist the College in developing new programs of study by providing information on the needs of specific industries/professions or developments in the community;
- Advise the College on the availability and suitability of community resources and industry support for work experience components of programs (e.g. co-op, clinical experience, field placement, summer employment and/or apprenticeship), and assist in recruitment of the placements for students, where possible;
- Provide input regarding community and industry trends that impact program outcomes and placements;
- Advise the College on suitability of resources such as facilities, laboratories and equipment as they relate to the learning process;
- Maintain an active public relations profile for the program and the college within industry and the community and ensure there is an ongoing public awareness of current and emerging career opportunities;

Source: OECD (2014b), "Employment and Skills Strategies in Canada", *OECD Reviews on Local Job Creation*, OECD Publishing.

schools to work intensively with those requiring support in this area. An additional instrument could be the creation of a network of vocational institution staff serving as a tool to transfer the knowledge and experiences of employers and VET working together. This type of support can be provided by regional and local centres for school development, potentially with the support of ESF.

Finally, due to a number of factors, including relatively low pay that makes it hard to recruit strong applicants and a stringent Charter of Teachers that makes it difficult to adjust staffing, stakeholders reported that VET teachers often have out of date skills and knowledge and there is little flexibility to adjust courses taught to labour market demands. While re-examining the national framework for VET teachers may be beneficial in the long-term (e.g. increasing pay or prestige of the position), in the shorter-term and at the local level, a number of other strategies could be used. This includes implementing measures to upgrade the skills and knowledge of existing teachers, for example through encouraging VET teachers to spend time in workplaces and participate in workplace training themselves (OECD, 2014c). Another complementary approach would be engaging more industry trainers in VET institutions. While their workplace and industry knowledge would be more up-to-date than teachers, they, on the other hand, may need more training around pedagogy and classroom and lab instruction. Such training may also be beneficial for workplace trainers who supervise apprenticeships. The box below provides an example of a programme in Finland that has created this type of virtuous circle between VET teachers and workplace trainers.

Box 4.5. **Telkkä programme in Finland**

The Telkkä programme in Finland offered vocational teachers the opportunity to undertake a two month on the job placement in which they were partnered with workplace trainers. For teachers, this provided the opportunity to update their professional skills, while workplace trainers had the opportunity to improve their pedagogical skills. Benefits reported by the teachers included updating workplace knowledge (familiarity with recent work practices and requirements and the equipment used) better networks and connections (which could be used to organise study visits, invite guest lecturers into the classroom), as well as increased confidence, motivation, and respect from students. The training period also gave teachers and workers the opportunity to discuss issues related to workplace training and improve training plans and assessment methods. The training period was complemented by a pre-training seminar to clarify goals. After the training, both teachers and workers were given the opportunity to provide feedback, which was synthesised across participants and disseminated to the broader community. The Economic Information Office in Finland has identified this programme as one of the best ways to develop teachers' professionalism.

Source: Cort, Härkönen and Volmari (2004), Field, S. et al. (2012), A Skills beyond School Review of Denmark.

Recommendation: Expand basic skills training opportunities

Despite a demonstrated need for basic skills training, there appears to be relatively few offerings in terms of basic skills development. Basic skills trainings are not common within training or VET institutions, or through poviat labour offices. There were some institutions in both case study areas offering courses at the level of gymnasium (ISCED 2a level) for adults. However, this training is more popular among relatively young people who had challenges finishing schools, rather than amongst older workers or jobseekers. Findings from this work as well as the OECD's 2016 Economic Survey of Poland both suggest a need for targeted interventions to improve basic skills.

While research on policy interventions to improve adult literacy and numeracy skills highlights the difficulties in designing successful programmes, a number of best practices can be drawn from the experiences of other OECD countries (Windisch, H.C. 2015) For one, outreach strategies that focus just on responding to existing demands, are unlikely to be successful, given that adults are often unable or unwilling to recognise their own basic skills weaknesses. Rather, outreach should seek to enhance motivation and awareness of the benefits of and opportunities to develop basic skills, targeting both the learners themselves as well as their employers, families and friends. Additionally, this research stressed that there is no "one-size fits all" approach, and rather programmes need to be tailored to the specific needs of particular learners. For example, the context of learning can matter significantly – some learners will respond to classroom based settings, while others may respond better to e-learning, work-based, or home- or community-based programmes. The box below provides examples of adult literacy and numeracy programmes that have used varying approaches.

Box 4.6. Examples of different approaches to improving adult literacy and numeracy

ICT-based-learning. ICT-based learning has the benefits of allowing for learning independent of class schedules and location, and can benefit learners who have had negative experiences with traditional classrooms or have physical access limitations. However, limited IT access or literacy as well as a lack of social contact means it is not suited for all learners.

For example, Learndirect is a network of online learning and information services which operates in England, Wales and Northern Ireland. It collaborates with further education colleges, private training providers, voluntary and community sector organisations and higher education institutions "to enable adults without a Level 2 or Skills for Life qualification to gain the skills and qualifications they need to find a job or to achieve and progress at work" (Broek, Buiskool and Hake, 2010). Learndirect has engaged over 2.6 million learners since 2000, and has hard particular success in reaching non-traditional learners (ECOTEC, 2001).

Provision in the workplace: Literacy and numeracy programmes delivered through the workplace can benefit both employers and employees, and can reach learners not typically involved in continuous education or training, including older workers.

In Denmark, for example, the adult education centre (VUC) in Southern Jutland owns two mobile classrooms in expandable lorries that have a capacity of 18 people each, as well as a camper classroom which holds fewer students. These mobile classrooms allow the VUC to deliver basic education classes on-site at the workplace. The classrooms are fully equipped for teaching, and class sessions are scheduled during the working day, so students can come directly to and from work. VUC has found that integrating the classes into the worksite motivates students, as they can see their colleagues going to class in their work clothes and hear them talking about class in the lunch break. For smaller companies that are not able to "release" a critical mass of employees for a class, VUC has also offered multi-company classes that are easily accessible for all participants.

Family literacy programmes: Recognising the strong intergenerational links between parents' and their children's literacy, family literacy programmes engage adults in their roles as parents as well as learners in their own rights.

One example is the Family Literacy Project in Hamburg, which has offered intergenerational family literacy programmes for children and parents from deprived social and migrant backgrounds since 2004. This programme has had a positive effect both on the parents and children involved (stronger family relationships and improved literacy skills) as well as on the kindergarten and school teachers, who have been able to enhance their intercultural teaching skills. The programme reaches about 1 000 parents and 1 000 children annually, and as a result of the project's success, many schools in Hamburg have established family literacy rooms where parents can meet.

Source: Windisch, H.C. (2015), "Adults with low literacy and numeracy skills: A literature review on policy intervention". Broek, S.D., B.J. Buiskool and B. Hake (2010), *Impact of ongoing reforms in education and training on the adult learning sector (2nd phase): Final Report.* Eurydices (2011), Adults in Formal Education: Policies and Practices. Tamkin, P., J. Hillage, S. Dewson, and A. Sinclair (2003), "New Learners, New Learning a strategic evaluation of Ufi". EU Lifelong Learning Programme (n.d.), *Literacy needs for vocational purposes in Europe. A documentation: facts, information and examples,* UNESCO (2014), "Family Literacy Project (FLY)".

Additionally, training and vocational courses focus on the development of technical skills, with less focus on developing advanced generic skills, such as co-operating, communication, team work, being creative and innovative, although all of them are important for employers, and in some cases even more important than purely technical skills. Therefore, the training programmes provided by both poviat labour offices and VET institutions should put more emphasis on the development of these types of skills. In many cases, this would require changes in how the courses are organised (such as more emphasis on team work and communication during the courses).

Targeting policy to local employment sectors and investing in quality jobs

Recommendation: Focus efforts on improving skills utilisation and work organisation

While much attention is given to the importance of job creation, it is also critical to consider the *type* and *quality* of jobs on offer in a local area. Additionally, investment in the supply of skills alone will not be sufficient to boost job creation and productivity in all local economies. The degree to which local employers are demanding and using skills also has to be taken into account. A low demand for skills among employers may mean that people's skills are not fully used or that workers have little incentive to upgrade their skills, knowing these skills will not be used in the jobs the local economy has to offer (OECD, 2014d).

Research also suggests a link between the way skills are used in the workplace and the potential for innovation. Countries with higher rates of work characterised by discretionary learning (high levels of autonomy in work combined with high levels of learning, problem-solving and task complexity) show higher levels of innovation while countries with more "taylorist" (low discretion and low level of learning and problem-solving) or "simple" forms of work organisation show lower levels of innovation. OECD research suggests that a bottleneck to improving the innovative capabilities of European firms might not be low levels of R&D expenditures, but rather the widespread presence of working environments that are unable to provide fertile grounds for innovation (OECD, 2010).

Recent OECD work on job quality shows that in 2014, Poland ranks in the bottom 10 of all OECD countries across the three key dimensions measured: earnings quality, labour market security, and quality of the working environment (OECD, 2016a). Additionally, as discussed earlier in this report, there is significant local variation in the demand for skills in Poland, but little policy interventions targeted towards improving skills utilisation. Finally, research into work organisation in the EU has shown that while discretionary learning in Poland is slightly higher than the EU average, it falls well below that of leading innovation countries, and actually has a higher rate of "simple" work organisation than the EU-28 average (Lorenz, 2015). A lack of high quality (or even formal) employment available to graduates of vocational schools was also raised as one reason this pathway is considered less prestigious. Taken together, these findings suggest a need to focus more on skills utilisation and work organisation with Polish employers.

Although Poland ranks highly in support for entrepreneurship skills in the Local Job Creation dashboard, this support tends to focus on supporting the "hard" skills of entrepreneurs, necessary to operate a business. As evidence proves that the productivity and development prospects of enterprises depend heavily on the quality of management, work organisation and skills utilisation, many enterprises in Poland could benefit from improvement and investment in developing these types of management skills, particularly small and medium firms.

There are new instruments supporting skills development: the National Training Fund, operated by poviat labour offices, and the European Social Fund, which in the current perspective (2014-20) will be more demand oriented. Both instruments should be used to improve skills utilisation and work organisation. New enterprises, which would like to receive financial support for skills development, could be required to prepare a plan for the improvement of skills and work organisation, with the support of the required counselling services. The plan could be based on an analysis of the needs and situation of the enterprise, and the supported skills development should be directly linked to this plan. Support for work organisation and skills utilisation could also be provided by other enterprises and employer organisations. This would require close co-operation with the main employer organisations in Poland. Two approaches to improving skills utilisation are discussed in the box below: one focusing on workplace organisation in Finland and one taking a sector approach in Australia.

Box 4.7. **Finland's workplace innovation programme**

"Liideri – Business, Productivity and Joy at Work Programme in Finland

Tekes, the Finnish funding agency for innovation runs a number of programmes to foster innovation, including "Liideri – Business, Productivity and Joy at Work Programme". Unlike more traditional innovation programmes, this programme focuses workplace development, in particular developing management practices and forms of working that promote the active utilisation of the skills and competences of employees. Liideri is the latest in a series of publicly funded workplace innovation programmes in Finland, which were first launched in 1993. While these programmes were initially coordinated through the Ministry of Labour, in 2008 they were transferred to Tekes (the Finnish Funding Agency for Technology and Innovation). This transfer was part of the adoption of a new national innovation strategy that emphasises demand and user-driven innovation and non-technological innovations.

The Liideri project has three focus areas: renewal of management; employee participation in renewal of products, services and their production; and new forms of work organisation and working. A number of instruments are used to effect change in these areas, including work organisation development projects, integrated R&D projects, funding for research, and widespread dissemination of the outcomes and principles of the work (websites, social media, case studies, workshops, network of experts, etc.)

National skills ecosystem projects in Australia

In Australia, national skills ecosystem projects were introduced in 2003. The skills ecosystem approach emphasises not just how skills are developed, but also how they are deployed. With this lens, perceived skills shortages can be attributed as much to work organisation and turnover challenges as to the supply of skilled people coming from education and training institutions. The projects covered areas such as VET links with research agencies to promote innovation, promoting new technology, workplace drivers of skill formation, skills formation to support the development of an industry cluster, and job design and career paths. Projects were ambitious and aimed to achieve long-term structural change.

While the national projects have since ceased, they had worthwhile impacts in specific industry sectors and the approach continues to inspire other skills initiatives. The dairy industry in the state of Victoria, in particular, approached an increasing demand for high-end skills using the skill ecosystem methodology and has used the process successfully. The shift in product market strategy from supplying traditional commodity based markets to value-added markets with all that this entailed (e.g. tighter product specifications, the introduction of new technologies, the development of participative workplaces, higher regulatory scrutiny, and higher levels of customer expectations) were the key drivers of a well-structured, industry-driven skills ecosystem for accelerating high-end skills development.

Source: Tekes (2014), Liideri – Business, Productivity and Joy at Work; a new Finnish National Programme, *www.workplaceinnovation.org/nl/kennis/kennisbank/liideri---business--productivity-and-joy-at-work--a-new-finnish-national-programme/1235*. Eddington, N. and P. Toner (2012), "Skills Formation Strategies in Queensland: A Skills Shortage?", *OECD Local Economic and Employment Development (LEED) Working Papers*, No. 2012/07, OECD Publishing, Paris, *http://dx.doi.org/10.1787/5k9b9mjdj4xr-en*.

Recommendation: Promote economic development that is inclusive and contributes to the creation of quality jobs, including through more strategic use of public procurement

In attracting investors, public policy should be more focused on supporting investments that provide large numbers of *quality* jobs, rather than just jobs in general. Attracting new investors providing a large number of decent jobs requires focused attention on the part of economic development actors, as well as investing in the best quality of initial and continuing vocational education and training. Close co-operation between the education and training sector can not only help ensure the development of in-demand skills, but also contribute to partnerships that further innovation through coordinated research and development projects. Both case study areas show that some strategic investment, with smart support from local authorities, could attract further investments and contribute to the further development of local enterprises and clusters. The box below provides two examples of local approaches to improving strengthening specific sectors and improving job quality.

Box 4.8. **Sectors, skills and quality jobs**

Attracting a new type of tourism in Blackpool, United Kingdom. Having long been a seaside resort that caters for high volume but low-spending customers, Blackpool is working hard to raise its game and attract higher spending customers through offering a higher quality "offer". The town has been growing its branded attractions (e.g. Madame Tussauds, Nikolodean, Merlin) while also investing significantly in infrastructure (trams, cycles, buying the Blackpool tower for the public, new concert hall, refurbished front). It is recognised that capital and infrastructure investments alone will be insufficient for realising the town's vision, and that alongside them there is a need for investment in skills, particularly in the area of customer service. This means investment in specific skills (for example, through local college courses geared to the tourism industry) but also more informal learning and knowledge sharing.

A particular emphasis has been placed on raising the aspirations of service personnel so that they project a better image of the town and at the same time become more committed both to Blackpool, their employers and their own personal career prospects. A good example of such an initiative is the Welcome to Blackpool Initiative funded initially by the Local Enterprise Growth Initiative (LEGI) introduced by the previous UK government. This project trains local people (especially those working in hospitality, leisure, tourism, transport and retail sectors, but also local residents) in appreciating the history of Blackpool, current developments and future plans. Through course attendance, participants learn more about Blackpool's attractions and services. The knowledge gained can then be used to enhance visitors' and local residents' experience of Blackpool. Employers have reported that the short course equips staff to deliver a high standard of customer service, which in turn impresses visitors to the town and encourages word of mouth recommendations and repeat visits to Blackpool. The initiative has shown that taxi drivers, those involved in tourism and local residents can be excellent ambassadors for Blackpool It was reported that over 3 000 people (of all ages) have attended the course in two years and that more than 250 organisations have benefited. Such initiatives have been useful in increasing staff retention in local firms, which traditionally have had high turnover rates, linked to the seasonality of tourism in the town. High turnover rates have been seen by some firms as representing a challenge in terms of investing in staff training and skills upgrading. Growing staff retention has allowed local employers such as the Sandcastle Water Park to start working with individuals on personal development plans.

Box 4.8. **Sectors, skills and quality jobs** *(cont.)*

Working with the retail sector in the municipality of Breda, Netherlands. Retail is an important part of the local economy of Breda in the Netherlands. The sector has 2 200 establishments in the area and is currently relatively stable. However, in the context of the ageing of the population it is expected that it will become more difficult to fill vacancies in the future. It is also acknowledged that more has to be done to increase the quality of employment in the sector and the productivity and competitiveness of local enterprises, particularly small and medium-sized enterprises (SMEs). Several organisations, such as the National Board for Retail Trade, the Retail Platform Breda, the Association of Enterprises in the city centre of Breda, the Chamber of Commerce and Werkplein Breda (a service to help people to access jobs which combines the public employment service and the local municipal social service department), have taken the initiative to establish a service unit for the retail sector (Servicepunt Detailhandel). The objective of this service unit is threefold:

- **Improving the inflow and outflow of workers and better managing labour market transitions within the sector:** for example, by improving the match between demand for labour and supply of labour through investments in skills
- **Training of staff:** implementing an external information and advice service on human resource management for SMEs to improve work organisation, productivity and the quality of local job opportunities
- **Improving the image of the sector:** stimulating and organising extra promotion with regard to working in the retail sector, improving customer satisfaction.

The strength of the service unit is that the approach is demand driven and based on one-on-one relationships with local retailers. If action is needed, this takes place immediately through individual company visits and visits to the members and board meetings of the association of retailers. Local work coaches (placing local people into work) also receive training from the National Board for Retail Trade.

In early 2010 a similar service point was established for the care and welfare sectors, with plans to develop one for technical professions. One consulted business representative felt that through this collaboration they have come a long way in a short period of time.

Source: Dorenbos, R. and F. Froy (2011), "Building flexibility and accountability into local employment services: Country report for the Netherlands", *OECD Local Economic and Employment Development (LEED) Working Papers*, No. 2011/13, OECD Publishing, Paris, *http://dx.doi.org/10.1787/5kg3mktqnn34-en*; Froy, F., S. Giguère and M. Meghnagi (2012), "Skills for competitiveness: A synthesis report", *OECD Local Economic and Employment Development (LEED) Working Papers*, No. 2012/09, OECD Publishing, Paris, *http://dx.doi.org/10.1787/5k98xwskmvr6-en*.

Another underused policy lever is the direct spending power of the public sector. Public authorities – local, regional and national – should strengthen the utilisation of public procurement and investment to promote quality job creation as well as create job and/or training opportunities for the unemployed and other disadvantaged groups. This would require a stronger emphasis on the social aspects of public procurement tenders, as well as strong support for this approach from national and regional authorities. Within national and EU regulations, there may be particular opportunities to consider how projects using EU structural funds can be strategically leveraged to support these types of social aims in addition to their other objectives.

Box 4.9. Using public procurement for social inclusion, city of Most, Czech Republic

The city of Most (Ústí nad Labem region) applied the condition that as part of four public contracts for the construction of flats in the Chanov quarter (a socially deprived locality) and one public contract for cleaning, 10% of all those hired had to be long-term unemployed. The cleaning services contract was awarded to a firm that hired one long-term unemployed person. Other long-term unemployed were also hired on short-term contracts. Candidates were put forward by local non-profit organisations and were mainly people with low levels of education, skills and work experience who, according to senior staff, were able and willing to learn. Five out of seven persons stayed in their job after completion of the contract and two were offered a permanent contract. The newly hired workers performed preparatory technical work, finishing and ancillary works.

Applying the 10% condition in tendering contracts did not burden bidders or make the contract more expensive for the city. The firms have been considering not only fulfilling the mandatory 10% quota but hiring other long-term jobless. The city of Most has incorporated the procurement terms into the Integrated Development City Plan and is considering how it can be applied to other contracts. The Agency for Social Inclusion has included the example of Most in a manual for municipalities to encourage them to take similar approaches.

Source: Agency for Social Inclusion (2012), "Guide for Municipalities", *www.socialni-zaclenovani.cz/prirucka*.

Recommendation: Ensure that adequate career guidance and information on pathways are available to both youth and adults, and that it is informed by local labour market assessments.

Most of the study participants agreed that there is a need to boost access to career guidance and improve its quality. This pertains to career guidance for young people and adults. In the case of young people, schools are obliged to provide career guidance. However, the law should clearly state the minimum amount of career guidance. The best results are achieved when there is a special structure (unit, group of teachers) responsible for providing these services and sufficient resources devoted to this task (time and persons). The second important aspect is the competence of persons providing these services. They should have the appropriate training and improve their skills in an ongoing manner. Thus, various opportunities for skills development should be created at the regional and local levels (e.g. training courses, networks, and on-line courses). Also, standards for career guidance and supporting material should be developed. This is a task that could be the responsibility of the National Centre for Supporting Vocational and Continuing Education.

Being inclusive

Recommendation: address gaps in services for most disadvantaged clients of public employment services

The recent reforms of the PES included a profiling system that classified clients into one of three groups: Stream I, Stream II, or Stream III. Stream III clients are those considered to be the farthest from the labour market and/or not ready to take up employment. The labour offices are considered not have the tools or resources to serve these clients, and thus the decision was taken to outsource support for these clients.

However, preliminary implementation results suggest significant challenges in the set-up of the current system. For one, it appears that there is little interest from social assistance centres, NGOs or private providers in running programmes for Stream III clients. Additionally, unlike Stream II clients, who can be served with a variety of instruments, the options for Stream III clients are much more limited. Some clients classified as Stream III could benefit from the instruments available to Stream II clients. Finally, the performance management system is focused on incentivising employment outcomes, without incentives for providing the other types of supportive services (e.g. wrap-around case management, mental health services, drug or alcohol counselling) that these clients may need before they are ready for stable employment. Overall, this leaves a major gap in the level and types of services available for the PES clients who may be most in need.

A number of approaches could help remedy this gap. For one, local PES staff could be given more discretion in moving clients from Profile III to Profile II where appropriate. The performance management incentives already in place could serve as one safeguard for ensuring that this is only done in cases where warranted. Additionally, the terms of the outsourcing arrangements for instruments used for Stream III clients may need to be revisited to make them more attractive to a broader range of potential providers. Performance measures for Stream III clients could also be adjusted to remove any disincentives to "bypass" necessary supports such as mental health counselling, etc.

Recommendation: Improve access to care services, particularly for children aged 0-3 years of age

The OECD's Economic Survey of Poland highlighted insufficient child care policies as a major structural weakness in the economy (OECD, 2014e; OECD, 2016b). There is still a large gap in access to childcare services for children younger than 3 years of age and those 3 years of age and older. This is particular the case in rural areas, but it is also an issue in larger cities, such as Poznań. The lack of affordable childcare services reduces the opportunities of parents, particularly women, on the labour market. This problem particularly concerns the youngest parents, at a low educational level or even during their education, who are not able to afford private childcare services.

The development of childcare services should focus on locally based, flexible forms of services, such as a daily nanny. This does not require a large investment and the scope of such services can quickly be adjusted to the actual demand. It can also provide job opportunities for older persons, who may be experiencing problems on the labour market.

The government has recognised the importance of developing affordable and quality child care services to increase the female labour market participation rate as well as to promote strong work-life reconciliation. Significant improvements have been made through a number of initiatives. Local governments have been encouraged to develop child care facilities and funding has been increased to subsidise more child care places for families. More efforts will need to continue build the child care infrastructure and to encourage flexible working arrangements. The government should encourage employers to adopt family friendly practices and seek to promote companies who are leaders in this area. Opportunities to build and better connect child care facilities to primary schools should be explored to build a seamless one-stop service for parents. Early years education and development is a critical determinant of future labour market success; therefore action must continue to develop a variety of child care arrangements.

References

Agency for Social Inclusion (2012), "Guide for Municipalities", *www.socialni-zaclenovani.cz/prirucka*.

Blien, U., F. Hirschenauer and P. thi Hong Van (2010), "Classification of Regional Labour Markets for Purposes of Labour Market Policy", *Papers in Regional Science*, Vol. 9, No. 4, November.

Broek, S.D., B.J. Buiskool and B. Hake (2010), *Impact of ongoing reforms in education and training on the adult learning sector (2nd phase): Final Report*, Research voor Beleid, *http://adultlearning-budapest2011.teamwork.fr/docs/Ongoing- Reforms-Adult-Learning-Final-Report.pdf*.

Cort, Härkönen and Volmari (2004) "PROFF – Professionalisation of VET teachers for the future", CEDEFOP, *www.cedefop.europa.eu/files/5156_en.pdf* .

Dorenbos, R. and F. Froy (2011), "Building flexibility and accountability into local employment services: Country report for the Netherlands", *OECD Local Economic and Employment Development (LEED) Working Papers*, No. 2011/13, OECD Publishing, Paris, *http://dx.doi.org/10.1787/5kg3mktqnn34-en*.

ECOTEC (2001), *Learndirect – A Comparative Study – A Final Report to the Department for Education and Employment*, ECOTEC, Birmingham.

Eddington, N. and P. Toner (2012), "Skills Formation Strategies in Queensland: A Skills Shortage?",*OECD Local Economic and Employment Development (LEED) Working Papers*, No. 2012/07, OECD Publishing, Paris, *http://dx.doi.org/10.1787/5k9b9mjdj4xr-en*.

EU Lifelong Learning Programme (n.d.), *Literacy needs for vocational purposes in Europe*. A documentation: facts, information and examples, Literacy and Vocation project, Zukunftsbau GmbH, Berlin.

European Commission (2013), *Review of Performance Management in Public Employment Services*, Brussels, Author: Alex Nunn.

European Commission (2012), *Performance management in Public Employment Services*, Brussels, Author: Alex Nunn.

Eurydices (2011), *Adults in Formal Education: Policies and Practices*, Brussels, Education, Audiovisual and Cultural Executive Agency, *http://eacea.ec.europa.eu/education/eurydice/documents/thematic_reports/128EN.pdf*.

Field, S. et al. (2012), *A Skills beyond School Review of Denmark*, OECD Reviews of Vocational Education and Training, OECD Publishing, Paris, *http://dx.doi.org/10.1787/9789264173668-en*.

Froy, F., S. Giguère and M. Meghnagi (2012), "Skills for competitiveness: A synthesis report", *OECD Local Economic and Employment Development (LEED) Working Papers*, No. 2012/09, OECD Publishing, Paris, *http://dx.doi.org/10.1787/5k98xwskmvr6-en*.

Lorenz, E. (2015), "Work Organisation, Forms of Employee Learning and Labour Market Structure: Accounting for International Differences in Workplace Innovation", *Journal of the Knowledge Economy*, 6(2), 437-466.

OECD (2016a), "Job quality", *OECD Employment and Labour Market Statistics* (database), *http://dx.doi.org/10.1787/e357cdbf-en* (accessed on 02 March 2016).

OECD (2016b), *OECD Economic Surveys: Poland 2016*, OECD Publishing, Paris, *http://dx.doi.org/10.1787/eco_surveys-pol-2016-en*.

OECD (2015), *OECD Employment Outlook 2015*, OECD Publishing, Paris, *http://dx.doi.org/10.1787/empl_outlook-2015-en*.

OECD (2014a), "Employment and Skills Strategies in the United States", *OECD Reviews on Local Job Creation*, OECD Publishing, Paris, *http://dx.doi.org/10.1787/9789264209398-en*.

OECD (2014b), "Employment and Skills Strategies in Canada", *OECD Reviews on Local Job Creation*, OECD Publishing, *http://dx.doi.org/10.1787/9789264209374-en*.

OECD (2014c), *Skills beyond School: Synthesis Report*, OECD Reviews of Vocational Education and Training, OECD Publishing, Paris, *http://dx.doi.org/10.1787/9789264214682-en*.

OECD (2014d), *Job Creation and Local Economic Development*, OECD Publishing, Paris, *http://dx.doi.org/10.1787/9789264215009-en*.

OECD (2014e), *OECD Economic Surveys: Poland 2014*, OECD Publishing, Paris, *http://dx.doi.org/10.1787/eco_surveys-pol-2014-en*.

OECD (2010), *Innovative Workplaces: Making Better Use of Skills within Organisations*, OECD Publishing, Paris, *http://dx.doi.org/10.1787/9789264095687-en*.

Skinner, G. (2012), "Department of Innovation, Business and Rural Development, Government of Newfoundland and Labrador", *OECD Conference*, October 2012, *www.oecd.org/rural/krasnoyarsk/3%20Gillian%20Skinner_MR2_Skill%20Building_ENG.pdf.*

Tamkin P., J. Hillage, S. Dewson and A. Sinclair (2003), "New Learners, New Learning a strategic evaluation of Ufi", DFES *Research Report* RR440, London, DfES.

Tekes (2014), Liideri – Business, Productivity and Joy at Work; A new Finnish National Programme, *www.workplaceinnovation.org/nl/kennis/kennisbank/liideri---business--productivity-and-joy-at-work--a-new-finnish-national-programme/1235.*

White House Council (2013), "Strong Cities, Strong Communities Initiative", *1st Annual Report, April 2013, www.huduser.org/portal/publications/pdf/huddoc.pdf.*

UNESCO (2014), "Family Literacy Project (FLY)", *www.unesco.org/uil/litbase/?menu=4&programme=67*, accessed 2 March 2016.

Windisch, H.C. (2015), "Adults with low literacy and numeracy skills: A literature review on policy intervention", *OECD Education Working Papers*, No. 123, OECD Publishing, Paris, *http://dx.doi.org/10.1787/5jrxnjdd3r5k-en.*

APPENDIX A

Results of survey to poviat labour offices

Section 1: Local collaboration

1. In addition to the local council, please indicate the intensity of your collaboration with the following organisations at the poviat level:

	No collaboration	Sharing information only	Some co-ordination of programmes and client services	Comprehensive joint programme/strategy development
Regional or local economic development agencies	31.3	42.3	12.5	13.9
Local government	1.0	21.2	23.6	54.3
Vocational schools	7.7	63.5	13.0	15.9
Post-secondary schools	21.6	60.1	7.7	10.6
State Higher School of Vocational Education)	32.7	43.3	9.6	14.4
Private or public training facilities	7.2	23.1	42.8	26.9
Universities	29.3	43.3	11.1	16.3
Employers	0.5	13.5	25.5	60.6
Private sector employment agencies	13.5	41.8	24.0	20.7
Non-government organisations working with disadvantaged populations (immigrants, disabled, ethnic minorities, etc.)	22.1	38.0	20.2	19.7
Welfare and social integration institutions (Social Assistance Centre, County Family Assistance Centre, Social economy entities)	3.4	13.5	25.5	57.7

Section 2: Working with employers

2. Does the training available locally (e.g. through PES, post-secondary schools and colleges) meet employer needs/demand for skilled workers? (please check applicable box with an x)?

No efforts are made to align training with local employer needs	1.0
Some efforts are made, but employers report significant problems with training not being aligned to their needs	3.4
Generally, training is geared towards meeting employer demand but improvements could still be made	67.3
Training is very well-aligned with the needs of employers	28.4

3. How often does your office/organisationzp conduct outreach with employers (please choose one from the list below by checking applicable box with an x)?

We have no communication with employers	0.5
We have infrequent communication with employers	1.0
We have some communication with employers but it could be improved	15.9
We have regular and frequent communication with employers	82.7

4. Who usually initiates the contact between your labour office and employers (please check applicable box with an x)?

Local labour office initiates contact	82.7
Employers initiate contact	17.3

5. Please indicate what types of employer engagement activities your office/organisation undertakes (please select all that apply by marking box with an x if applicable):

Conduct outreach to see what job opportunities are available	89.4
Place unemployed individuals into local job opportunities (vacancies)	98.1
Promote apprenticeships and other work-based training opportunities	94.7
Provide clear career pathways between training and local work opportunities	79.3
Providing training to upskill existing employers' current employees	82.2
Advise employers on better human resources/workplace organisation management	31.2

Section 3: Targeting disadvantaged groups

6. Are there specific employment programmes delivered by your office designed to meet the needs of local disadvantaged groups?

	Yes
Older workers	96.6
Youth	98.1
Women	84.6
Immigrants	6.7
Ethnic minorities	7.7
Long-term unemployed	97.6
People with disabilities	96.2
Displaced Workers	57.7

Section 4: Adjusting programmes to regional and local needs

7. In your opinion, what is the level flexibility available at the local level in managing programmes and services?

On a scale from 1-4, please put 1 if you have no flexibility (i.e., completely centrally determined) and 4 if you have high flexibility (i.e., local level has complete freedom to determine)

	No flexibility	Limited flexibility	Some flexibility	High flexibility
Programme and strategy design	6.3	18.8	45.2	29.8
Budget management	6.7	16.3	46.6	30.3
Performance management	12.5	38.5	38.9	10.1
Choice of target groups/eligibility criteria	13.5	30.3	37.0	19.2
Contracting/outsourcing arrangements	27.4	25.0	27.9	19.7

8. Recently a new law on promotion of employment and institutions of labour market was introduced. To what extent did the new regulation increase your flexibility in delivering programmes and services.

	No increase	Minimal increase	Some increase	Significant increase
Programme and strategy design	13.5	27.9	40.9	17.8
Budget management	12.0	31.7	40.9	15.4
Performance management	23.1	37.0	31.3	8.7
Choice of target groups/eligibility criteria	17.8	36.5	31.3	14.4
Contracting/outsourcing arrangements	25.0	37.5	25.5	12.0

9. If your office was to have greater flexibility in delivering programmes and services, where would you find this most useful?

	Not useful	A little useful	Somehow useful	Very useful
Programme and strategy design	6.3	17.3	33.7	42.8
Budget management	6.7	19.7	38.0	35.6
Performance management	9.1	30.3	34.1	26.4
Choice of target groups/eligibility criteria	8.2	18.3	35.6	38.0
Contracting/outsourcing arrangements	16.8	33.7	32.2	17.3

10. In your opinion, does your organisation have sufficient financial and human resources to achieve its goals? Please rank each from 1 - insufficient to 4 - fully sufficient

	Not at all sufficient	Somewhat sufficient	Adequate	Fully sufficient
Financial resources	15.9	26.4	40.4	17.3
Staffing levels	25.0	32.7	33.2	9.1
Skills of employees	0.5	4.8	48.1	46.6
Labour market knowledge of staff	0.5	4.8	48.1	46.6

ORGANISATION FOR ECONOMIC CO-OPERATION AND DEVELOPMENT

The OECD is a unique forum where governments work together to address the economic, social and environmental challenges of globalisation. The OECD is also at the forefront of efforts to understand and to help governments respond to new developments and concerns, such as corporate governance, the information economy and the challenges of an ageing population. The Organisation provides a setting where governments can compare policy experiences, seek answers to common problems, identify good practice and work to co-ordinate domestic and international policies.

The OECD member countries are: Australia, Austria, Belgium, Canada, Chile, the Czech Republic, Denmark, Estonia, Finland, France, Germany, Greece, Hungary, Iceland, Ireland, Israel, Italy, Japan, Korea, Luxembourg, Mexico, the Netherlands, New Zealand, Norway, Poland, Portugal, the Slovak Republic, Slovenia, Spain, Sweden, Switzerland, Turkey, the United Kingdom and the United States. The European Union takes part in the work of the OECD.

OECD Publishing disseminates widely the results of the Organisation's statistics gathering and research on economic, social and environmental issues, as well as the conventions, guidelines and standards agreed by its members.

LOCAL ECONOMIC AND EMPLOYMENT DEVELOPMENT (LEED)

The OECD Programme on Local Economic and Employment Development (LEED) has advised governments and communities since 1982 on how to respond to economic change and tackle complex problems in a fast-changing world. Its mission is to contribute to the creation of more and better quality jobs through more effective policy implementation, innovative practices, stronger capacities and integrated strategies at the local level. LEED draws on a comparative analysis of experience from the five continents in fostering economic growth, employment and inclusion. For more information on the LEED Programme, please visit *www.oecd.org/cfe/leed*.

OECD PUBLISHING, 2, rue André-Pascal, 75775 PARIS CEDEX 16
(84 2016 04 1 P) ISBN 978-92-64-25549-4 – 2016

www.ingramcontent.com/pod-product-compliance
Ingram Content Group UK Ltd.
Pitfield, Milton Keynes, MK11 3LW, UK
UKHW051241300926
15471UKWH00015B/1458

9 789264 255494